24 Reasons
Why African Americans
Suffer

by Jimmy Dumas

Chicago, Illinois

Front cover illustration by Tony Quaid
Copyright © 1999 by Jimmy Dumas
First Edition, First Printing

Printed in the United States of America

ISBN: 0-913543-63-2

Contents

Acknowledgments

This message of thanks is for those individuals who helped make this book a reality. The following people inspired me when I was down. They would not let me give up, even when I was tempted to throw in the towel. They are. . .

Roderick L. Dumas
Mary Dumas Andrews
Virginia Walton
Millie Steele
Pamela Walton
Constance Palmer
Mr. and Mrs. George Scott
Ruben Davis
Anthony Dumas
Charles Eric Dumas
Robert "Bob" Kent
Herman Jiles, Jr.
William A. Moore
John W. Brooks, Esq.
Irwin Prince, Esq.
Louis Rayford
Denise Gavia-Currin
Mamie Pantillion
Mr. and Mrs. James Nobles
Mr. and Mrs. Leonard Burroughs
Melissa Kittrell

If there's anyone else I neglected to include in this public acknowledgment, please forgive. I am grateful to each and every one of you.

Introduction: An Open Letter to African Americans

Dear Brothers and Sisters:

Have you ever heard the expression, "The best defense is a good offense?" Coaches, corporate executives, and others often use offensive strategies to ensure that their team wins the game. Unfortunately, we African Americans have not learned the value of a good offense, nor have we learned offensive tactics. But if our goal is to win at life, we must begin to learn how to play the game more intelligently and more aggressively. Most important, we must have faith in our ability to play and win.

We have been playing defense since the first day of our forced arrival on American soil. We have been defending ourselves against enemies both seen and unseen, against obstacles both universal and those specifically directed against our race and culture. Have our strategies been effective? Read a newspaper or watch the evening news. Record levels of incarceration, substance abuse, and poverty beset our community. Despite civil rights legislation of the '60s, we do not have equal access to quality health care, education, and housing. Male-female relationships are in crisis, and most of our children are being raised by one parent, usually the mother.

In the Art of War, Sun Tzu said that to win the war you must first know your enemy. After nearly 400 years, we think we know the opposition, but our knowledge has been tainted by centuries of slavery and racism. Our relationship with him has even subverted our knowledge of ourselves and our genius. Because we believe his ways are superior to ours, we are constantly confused and defeated by him. The opposition's lukewarm, superficial offense is nothing against our stubborn lack of confidence and faith in ourselves. But the contrary is true too. The opposition *cannot* win against our confidence in ourselves and faith in God. Nor can he win against our *unified* offense.

Many messengers of truth have tried to tell us that constantly playing defense is begging for a loss. Time and again they have said, "The best defense is a good offense." Put another way, we must become proactive rather than reactive. We must learn how to put our opponent into a defensive posture, and then keep him on the run. Let him react to *our* vision, *our* goals, *our* initiatives, *our* focused and disciplined action.

The best teams are led by individuals of great vision. To whom will African Americans turn for leadership?

In whom will we put our trust? Who is the one superstar that will lead our efforts? Where will the superstar come from? How much will his contract cost? How long will his contract run? How will he pass the baton to future generations?

Over the centuries God has blessed us with men and women of great vision and courage. From Nat Turner and Harriet Tubman to Malcolm X and Martin Luther King, the superstars of our race have lead us in offensive attacks against the opposition. Thanks to them, we have had shining moments of victory.

Through the church, we have access to the greatest Superstar, God Almighty. During four centuries of American captivity, we turned to God for relief from our opponent's constant siege. We turned to Him through praying, singing, sharing, caring, and loving one another. And God carried us through one catastrophe after another until freedom was won.

The one institution in our community that is in a strong offensive position to lead us out of our suffering is the African American church. Then why, as the comptrollers of a wealth so vast that it rivals the bottom line of many of the world's largest corporations, is the African American church *as a whole* failing to make the much needed offensive plays? There are some churches devoted to healing our families, developing our economy, teaching our children—as well as attending to our spiritual needs—but the examples are far and few in between.

At this time, the African American church, with its current structure and leadership, does not have the capacity to lead us out of our misery. Its present structure, with its deacon boards, pastor as sole proprietor, associations, conferences, conventions, and national organizations, does not, nor was it ever intended to fight poverty with spiritual force. The present structure of the African American church lends itself to graft, petty and grand theft, lack of sound business practices, and disorganization. Too many of its leaders are egocentric, arrogant, uneducated, and sleeping with the enemy and the flock. Too many use religion as a psychological whip to beat a people who are already down. Their own unresolved spiritual and emotional issues undermine their ability to serve, and this is a sin.

The African American church must change. No longer can it continue to misappropriate the tithes and offerings of its members. This is God's money, and it must be used for God's holy purposes. Today's church pastors, ministers, and lay people must reclaim the vision of early church leaders. Funds that are given in good faith must be used to benefit community initiatives in education, finance, health, housing, and family.

The African American church is a house divided, and a house divided against itself cannot stand. We are split apart by warring factions, a problem I call "denominationalism." We must all begin the difficult, yet necessary, process of healing our differences, agreeing to disagree, and moving forward in order to unite across denominational lines.

I propose that African American churches unite under a common umbrella, with each contributing a minimum of $20.00 per week. This will create a strong economic base out of which we can begin to heal the sick, feed the hungry, create new businesses, educate children, and heal families. The African American church and its congregations must get in step and unite today. Start now! Become proactive now!

One organizational prototype that can serve as a model of African American church unity is the Congress of National

Black Churches, Inc. Founded in 1978 by Bishop Roy L. H. Winbush (African Methodist Episcopal), Bishop John Hurst Adams (African Methodist Episcopal), and representatives of other denominations, the purpose of this organization is to bring together Black religious leaders to dialogue across denominational lines. Its ecumenical coalition consists of eight historically Black denominations: African Methodist Episcopal; African Methodist Episcopal Zion; Christian Methodist Episcopal; Church of God in Christ; National Baptist Convention of America, Inc.; National Baptist Convention, USA, Inc.; National Missionary Baptist Convention of America; and Progressive National Baptist Convention, Inc. Together, these denominations represent 65,000 churches and a membership of more than 20 million people.[1] Their efforts are to be commended.

We must work with the Congress of National Black Churches to create the economic stability that we need to survive. If each one of the 85,000 member churches assumed responsibility for incubating one business which would then hire one employee, then 85,000 people would be removed from the unemployment roles. The weekly contribution of $20.00 per week would generate $885 million for community renewal and development initiatives. I know I am dreaming, but this is not impossible. It can and must be done.

The African American church cannot shoulder the entire blame for our problems, however. If we are to truly understand our predicament, we must revisit the most painful period in our recent history—slavery. Needless to say, slavery was detrimental to us in nearly every way. African Americans were the only race of people brought to America as slaves, against their will. Our forefathers and foremothers were disrespected, oppressed, and brutalized. After hundreds of years of enslavement and following the 1863 Civil War, we were turned loose, not set free as the history books have proclaimed.

Charles H. Wesley, in his introduction to the *International Library of Negro Life and History*, says that

> "When the Civil War ended the Nation faced a number of new problems. A major one was the plight of the four million freedmen, who had to be provided with jobs, housing and education . . .The period of transition from war to peace did not provide for any systematized settlement of these black people, and many of them wandered over the countryside seeking a livelihood where they could find it."[2]

Our present day instability and lack of unity have their roots in the lack of post Civil War planning, and we still lack a plan today. Let us begin the planning process by reading this book. My goals in writing *24 Reasons Why African Americans Suffer* are to provide food for thought and some positive, proactive, offensive strategies for the empowerment of our people. Any organization can use the strategies presented in this book to develop a plan that will deliver us from substandard, mediocre living.

As you can see, the problems that faced our ancestors in 1863 are still with us today. The race issue will always be with us, but don't despair. We can use it to bring us together.

Reason 1—Lack of Unity

It is widely believed that African Americans do not, will not, cannot, nor will they ever stick together to accomplish anything worthwhile. Everyone believes it and so do we.

In his *Introduction to Black Studies*, Maulana Karenga states that five strategies were used to control slaves. Strategy #4—disrupting and forbidding unity among slaves—had the devastating effect of obliterating African culture, memories, and consciousness.[1] Instead of unity, arbitrary divisions based on hue, gender, and class separated us, and these divisions remain with us today. While we have not stopped playing together, partying together, dancing together, or loafing on street corners together, we seem unable to come together for the important work of building our community.

We must come together for the good of the individual as well as the group. Without love, trust, and respect for one another, we will not be able to effectively educate our children or build our economy. However, respect for others begins with respect for self. If you do not know that your heritage is a great one and that greatness is your birthright, then you will believe the lies of our opponents. Self-respect can be developed by studying the Bible from an African-centered perspective and the great works of African-centered scholars. Then and only then we will be able to effectively unite with other African Americans.

Historical Examples of African American Unity

When African Americans come together for a common cause, we can accomplish great things. The sit-ins and the March on Washington in the 1960s and the million marches for men, women, and youth of the 1990s were great illustrations. As a race, we've been at our best when challenged by a crisis. Let us learn from and be inspired to take unified action by the historical record.

The Montgomery Bus Boycott, 1955. The Montgomery Bus Boycott, led by Dr. Martin Luther King, made the greatest impact on race relations in this country. Today, we take riding on public transportation for granted, but many African Americans who are alive today still remember what it was like to ride on a bus during the era of Jim Crow segregation. Not only did Black people have to ride at the back of the bus, if no seats were available, they had to stand up. If the bus reached capacity, they had to get off to make room for White riders, whether or not they had reached their destination.

African Americans were tired of such mistreatment, but nothing changed until one woman, Rosa Parks, refused to stand up because her feet hurt. This one act mobilized our race to unite and fight against racism and injustice.

1998 Congressional Election. In November 1998, African Americans used their voting power to dash Republican hopes of increasing representation in the Congress. The Democrats' strong presence in all levels of government is due in great measure to Blacks voting as a unified block. *USA Today* reported that from 1982 to 1996, the Democrats averaged 86.25 percent of the Black vote.[2]

If we are still alive for the presidential election in November 2000, African Americans will send the voting message of all time to America and the world: Any and all public officials not attuned to the needs and desires of African Americans will be removed from office by the almighty vote. I believe that African American voter turnout in the first year of the new millennium will exceed any voter turnout in history. You heard it here first.

Mandates for Unity

So we know we can vote, protest, and boycott, but can we come together to make money and build a strong Black economy? We did, once. In 1900, Booker T. Washington invited prosperous African American business owners from across the country to meet to discuss the formation of a national organization. According to Charles Wesley, 400 business leaders from 34 states met in Boston to form the Negro Business League.[3] If we did it then, we can do it again.

We have everything we need to develop unity around economic issues. Love, respect, and our love of God can withstand any attack. We have the power to move against poverty, unemployment, poor education and health care, and all the other ills that face our community.

We teach our children to stand up to bullies. Some of us even tell our children that if they don't, they'll get another beating at home. Yet, when it comes to the offensive plays waged against us by racists and their institutional racism, we take our beatings like a terrified child. We cannot tell our children one thing and then behave in a contrary way. This is a mixed message that, at present, has us all confused.

Rosa Parks did not let the riders, bus driver, or police bully her into giving up her seat. Only when she was arrested did she condescend to leave quietly. We must unite in that same courageous spirit and fight back against bigotry. When you keep taking your beating without fighting back, the bully will continue his war against you. But when you fight back, he learns to respect you, and he will not bother you again.

The Economic Roundtable. We will take our share of the American Dream when we come together to plan and build. Do not believe the lie that working together is reverse racism. Other races and ethnic groups work together. Why shouldn't we?

The purpose of the Economic Roundtable would be to discuss and plot the path of African Americans into the next century. We must become knowledgeable about market research, accounting practices, and trends in technology. We spend inordinate amounts of money in a variety of industries, and it's our turn to capitalize on the bottom line. Some of the industries that we must begin to investigate and eventually dominate are pharmacology, medicine, technology, transportation (service and manufacturing), textiles, entertainment, and telecommunications. Wherever we spend our money, that's where our greatest minds and builders should be.

According to the June 1, 1999 U.S. Census Bureau report, there are 34,895,000 African Americans living in America.[4] Imagine the impact we could make if only ten percent came together with the goal of economic prosperity for African Americans. We'd be unbeatable!

Come Together

Occasionally, during times of extreme stress, we have shown the world that we are serious about our own survival.

Today, we are faced with some of the greatest challenges to our sanity and survival. What will we do about it? Here are some suggestions:

1. Boycott one product (gym shoes, for example) for a period of ninety days or more.
2. Convene an economic think tank that will brainstorm, plan, and incubate African American businesses.
3. Conduct a worldwide "love in," in which all peoples of color would lay down their weapons and vow to never use them against one another again.

We Can and We Must!

Surely, we can do more than dance, sing, and party together. Let's unite to produce this cultural shock wave that will be heard and felt around the world. African American unity on a major scale will give the notorious media something worthwhile to discuss, rather than rehashing Black crime, poverty, and welfare statistics.

Where there is unity there is strength. Unite now or be destroyed.

Reason 2—Poor Money Management

African Americans are at the height of their economic earning potential. At no other time in our history has our earned income been as high as it is today. Sure there are many of us still struggling on skid row, in the ghetto, and on welfare, but the numbers of African Americans in the middle class and beyond are climbing. According to the Census Bureau, African Americans were the only race to experience an increase in real median income between 1993 and 1994. Our median income rose from $24,021 to $25,050, an increase of 4.3 percent.[1]

Given our increasing earning power, the most important questions of the day are. . .

- ♦ With whom will we spend our money?
- ♦ How will we increase our income?
- ♦ How will we manage our personal finances?

We hardly spend any of our disposable income within our own neighborhoods. We refuse to save. We do not put our money in Black banks. We refuse to support Black businesses. We are committing suicide!

Simple Solutions

The solutions are simple. We must support Black businesses. We must shop at the Black-owned clothing stores, record shops, and grocery stores in our own neighborhoods. We must become much more disciplined about saving and investing our money.

Save or invest a minimum of ten percent of your income in a minority bank. This is how we will build economic power. There is no limit to what we can accomplish if we begin to save with Black banks. We must stop being the bottom line for every bank and major corporation in America except our own. According to Wesley,

> Late in the Reconstruction Era, Negroes also began to establish banking houses. The Rev. W. W. Browne headed the first great effort of the Negro to organize a bank—an effort resulting in the formation of the Savings Bank of the Grand Fountain of the Order of True Reformers, in Richmond (Virginia). The Bank opened in April 1899 with $100,000 in capital. Some twenty eight banks were founded by Negroes between 1889 and 1900. Most were short lived; none survives today. Negro fraternal orders, benefit societies and churches wielded a vital influence in these undertakings. They wanted depositories for their funds, and felt that the establishment of Negro Banks for that purpose would benefit the entire Negro community.[2]

Nothing has changed. We still need to control our own dollars in our own banks. Do you even know who controls the bulk of Black wealth? Unfortunately, it's not us. It's sad, but we don't control our own money.

Dennis Kimbro says in his book, *Think and Grow Rich: A Black Choice*,

> Black America, you are already rich! In case you have fallen for the nonsense that blacks are poor, consider this not-so-well known fact: Black Americans earn $500 billion a year on goods and services.

This dollar figure is equivalent to the gross national product of Canada or Australia, two of the ten largest nations in the free world. Black America's problem is not a lack of money; its problems stem from what it does with the money it has.[3]

Create a Family Fund. All too often, Blacks live from paycheck to paycheck, and when crises strike, we're stuck. The purpose of the Family Fund is to have a pool of liquid cash for emergencies or the everyday needs of your immediate family. It can also be a savings or money market account in which you put a certain amount, usually every month. This fund can be used for maintenance and repairs, medical emergencies, tuition and fees, or any other financial need. Meet and decide how much to save and how to spend the money. Once you've decided, stick to your plan. If the money is for education, don't use it to buy clothes or go on a vacation. Sometimes we do that and never replace the funds. Maintain discipline with your Family Fund. Consider this money sacred to the financial security of your family.

Every family has at least one person who is good at managing money. Make sure that this account is managed by someone who understands and appreciates the value of money, preferably the patriarchal or matriarchal head.

Also, consider a joint venture with other Black families. Whether your Fund includes money from one family or more, make sure that the rules are agreed upon by everyone and that regular meetings are conducted.

Regardless of your family's income, you can begin to put even a small amount away today. For example, has every employed adult in your household donate a minimum of $5.00 per month. Place the funds in an interest-bearing account (in a Black bank or Black-managed fund).

As your Fund grows, you might consider investing it or allocating a portion to a trust account to benefit future generations. Like they say, if you don't plan, then plan to fail. Black people are notorious for not planning beyond the immediate needs of the moment. Leaving a legacy is a very important concept in the African world view. The Family Fund is one way to leave a positive legacy that will ensure a quality future for your children.

Teach your children—the younger the better—how to make and manage money. Someone once said that poverty is the worst kind of violence. "30 percent of Black children live in families with incomes below 50 percent of the federal poverty threshold."[4] More than a million of our children are growing up in poverty, despite our collective $350 billion. Instill in your children a healthy appreciation for what money can do for they will be responsible for their own prosperity or poverty when they get older. Give them a fighting chance. Teach them that money is not evil; it's the *love* of money that's evil. Money can be used to build or destroy. Teach them even while they are still in the womb.

The moment they begin to earn their own money, show them how to save and open up their own savings account. Have them allocate a reasonable dollar amount as savings, and follow-up with them regularly to make sure they are sticking to it. Teach them about the power of compound interest on their funds.

Teach them the importance of tithing a tenth of their income. Giving to church and community instills in children a sense of responsibility that goes beyond their own immediate needs. Become a model of discipline. Show, through your own behavior, how to set financial goals and stick to them.

Don't rely on the educational system to teach your children about economics. Learn yourself, then teach your children, and teach them from an African-centered perspective. We already know a lot about supply and demand, especially demand. We spend so much money on frivolous things that we barely have enough at the end of the month to keep the lights on. Give them a healthy, balanced, African-centered perspective of acquiring material goods. While there's nothing wrong with having a nice car or clothes, there is something wrong if you're spending way beyond your ability to pay. Do not leave your children a legacy of debt and bondage.

Our young people have gotten the wrong idea about the self-esteem–money–material goods connection. Puff Daddy raps, "It's all about the benjamins, baby," but it's not. Economic empowerment is about more than just money. It's about what we can do as a community with the money we have to take responsibility for our own lives, to build our own institutions, to educate our children, and to heal our sick. When you live from paycheck to paycheck, it is difficult to respect yourself. But when you take control of your finances, you develop self-worth. Stress is lowered and the quality of life is enhanced. You help yourself and your family, and you are in a position to help other people. You can make a difference without money, but with money, you can change the world.

Own property. "According to the National Association of Realtors (nar.realtor.com), the market is quite strong. Sales of existing single-family homes are expected to increase 3.2% to a total of 4.35 million units in 1998."[5] Congratulations to all the African American property owners in this country. In our neighborhoods, there are plenty of vacant lots, homes, apartment buildings, storefronts, and office spaces available to purchase, yet, ownership remains woefully low among African Americans.

Unfortunately, this has widened the gap between the Black haves and the Black have-nots. Property ownership has created a class system among us. Property owners often succumb to feelings of elitism, the "I am better than you" syndrome. Some Black property owners are no better than the landlords of other races who greatly contributed to the demise of many inner city neighborhoods. Worse, many of us don't keep up our own homes. Even if you cannot afford to renovate your property, you can afford to keep it clean. There is no excuse for littered lawns and graffiti on garages. If you own it, you must take care of it.

A home is more than just a home; it is an investment. Do you know that the home that you own can be used as collateral for a business loan? Once you've gone through the hard work of becoming approved for a mortgage (and it can be tough), you're in a financial position to do much more than you ever imagined. Begin to educate yourself about the true meaning of home ownership. We exist in a capitalistic society in which people and things can be leveraged to make even more money. That's the name of the game, and we Black people must learn how to play if we are to become powerful in the next century.

Young people, your first real estate purchase should be a wealth building duplex or quadruplex. Live in one unit and lease out the others at a price high enough to cover the cost of your unit. That way, you don't have to pay rent. Your money is freed up to invest in other projects or even buy other buildings. Invest the money that you would have paid for rent and an additional ten percent for 20 years or more. Many wealthy African Americans began in just this way. Don't get caught up in the trick bag of living from paycheck to paycheck. Financial worry is the number one destroyer of African American marriages. Save yourself some trouble. Strive for financial freedom. Be disciplined, and you'll never have to worry about your future.

We must design and implement plans to repair our communities. Let us work together to eliminate slums from the inner city. Like Pastor Floyd Flake of Allen A.M.E. Church says, "You see a ghetto, but I see paradise." We have incredible wealth in our midst, but we lack the vision. It's a challenge to see a mansion on a vacant lot, an elegant office building instead of a transient hotel, a beautiful park instead of a lot littered with alcohol cans, broken glass, and garbage. But I challenge you, use your imagination. Begin to dream big for your people and your community. See yourself regaining, retaining, repairing, recycling, renovating, and rebuilding. See your neighbors creating jobs, enhancing skills, and buying property.

In his book *Economic Empowerment Through the Church, Neighborhood Revitalization*, Gregory J. Reed says, "Neighborhood revitalization through the implementation of housing rehabilitation programs often serves as the cornerstone for church community development corporations. Churches in urban areas, in particular, have taken advantage of this tool to promote neighborhood stabilization around their boundaries."[6]

When you buy property, you must be prepared to take care of it. Landscaping, building maintenance, and upgrades are critical to increasing its value. Even beautifying the facade of a property is important. We must do whatever it takes to keep the property value appreciating. According to *Black Enterprise*, "the national median home price this spring was $128,200, up 6.2% from a year ago."[7] Your efforts to beautify and modernize your home will be realized when you're ready to sell.

A word of warning: Don't expect buying property to be easy. Discrimination is still a factor in Blacks being turned down for loans. The Association of Community Organizations for Reform Now study shows that from 1995 to 1997, minorities were rejected for home mortgages at a higher rate than Whites. "Nearly 3 percent of mortgage applications by Blacks were rejected in 1997, up from 25 percent in 1995. Blacks were 210 percent more likely than Whites to be rejected in 1997, up from 207 percent in 1995. The study also found that minorities received a higher rate of government-backed mortgages, suggesting they are steered to loans that can be easier, the Association said."[8]

Cars. African Americans love their cars. They give us prestige and status. More than one brother has "caught" a sister because of the car that he was driving.

But what do we know about the industry that designs, manufactures, markets, and sells cars? What do we know about our own cars? The next time you consider buying a car, ask yourself the following questions:

- In what country was your prospective car manufactured?
- What is the size of your prospective car's engine?
- Will your prospective car hold its resale value?
- At what point in the life of your prospective car will it become a liability?
 - What is the manufacturer's record regarding the hiring and promoting of Black people?

The last question is of utmost importance to African Americans. Even in our so-called enlightened age of racial equality, Blacks in the automotive industry still can't get a break. For example, *USA Today* reports that in 1999 the automobile industry honored, for the first time, an African American dealer. For 87-year-old Ed Davis, being inducted into the Automotive Hall of Fame was a long time in coming.

Ed Davis got his first job as a car salesman in 1937. But because he was black, he was banned from the showroom and had to meet customers in a converted second-floor supply room. Even so, he out sold all the other salesmen.

In 1939, Davis became the first African American car dealer, selling Studebakers. He later sold Chrysler-Plymouth vehicles in Detroit until retiring in 1971. Thursday, January 7, 1999, about 2000 auto industry leaders, including CEO's of major companies, paid tribute to Davis, 87, during the North American International Auto Show. A Scholarship fund was established in his name to help black students get auto industry jobs. Davis, is one of only 10 dealers, and the first African-American, inducted into the Automotive Hall of Fame. Looking back over his groundbreaking career, he said: "It was tough. Banks wouldn't loan you any money, and sometimes it was hard to get people to work for you."[9]

Since there are no Black car manufacturers (yet), we must focus our buying power and support African American car dealers. Seek out a Black car dealer and take your business to him.

Often, when the issue of buying Black is raised, many of our people will say, "I work hard for my money and I will spend it anyway I please." You are free to spend your money anyway you please, but every dime that is spent outside our community is a leak in our cumulative wealth. Every dime that is spent to support Black business is building our wealth. To understand my point requires a communal way of thinking that goes beyond petty, selfish individualism.

Imagine if Americans took their hard earned money and spent it in other countries. America would sink into poverty. Economists would be saying, America is the richest country in the world, but there are no institutions. The people are cash poor. Why don't they support their own entrepreneurs? In other words, they would be saying exactly the same things I'm telling you in this book. Ethnic Americans support their own. When will we learn?

The only way that we will become wealthy as a nation is to support our own—even if that means spending a few extra dollars on a product that you could have gotten cheaper downtown. If you do not spend in the community, you are against the community. If you do not support your brothers and sisters, you are supporting people who don't look like you and who don't respect you. If you do not support Black businesses, one day the chickens will come home to roost. One day White people may not want to hire you, not even to clean their toilets. Like Rev. Flake says, affirmative action is on the respirator. They don't have to hire you or educate you anymore. Where will you turn? To the Black businesses you've refused to support? How do you know they'll exist? You, and many other African Americans, have refused to help build them up!

African American car dealers are doing business in a very racist industry, and they need our support. It took Ed Davis to reach 87 years old before he could see his life's work recognized by the industry, and he's the only Black to be so recognized. There are many more African American car dealers. Will we have to wait another century before another dealer gets his due?

Many African Americans work for the car industry in union level positions. In other words, we do not hold a significant number of management positions. Still, the creation of the African American middle class can be credited, in part, to the automotive industry. According to Wesley, as Black laborers abandoned farm work and migrated North, many got well paying jobs in car factories.[10]

Unfortunately, our representation even at the union level is slipping. *Black Enterprise* reports that "Collectively, the Black Enterprise Auto Dealer list experienced a 6.2% decline in sales growth, from $5.93 billion in 1996 to $5.55 billion in 1997. And, 9,111 employees received paychecks from the BE Auto Dealer 100 List—a 1.05% decrease from the previous year."[11]

To Buy or Not to Buy?

When presented with the choice of whether to buy a car or a house, the answer should not be difficult. Buy a house. Property appreciates in value. Except for the rare exception, cars don't. But, because many of us do not have a plan for our finances, we are led by emotion to not only buy the car, but the most expensive car. How many of us are living in our cars right now because we put all our hard earned dollars in one basket? Once, an expensive foreign car was seen chained to the front porch of an African American family's house. The car was three times the value of the house. Whom were they trying to impress?

No one is trying to begrudge you a nice car, but try and get some balance on this issue. Think of your financial future. The high monthly note, insurance, and maintenance costs, not to mention weekly gas fill ups, will drain you of a sizable portion of your income. Are you really ready to commit to such a tremendous outlay of cash? Most important, is it necessary? Can you get by with a less prestigious but well-made car that costs less?

Clothes

As my friend Ray Ford often says, "The rich and famous image African Americans portray is not the true image they really are." And what enhances the image even more than a car? That's right, *clothes*.

Individually, we are the poorest of all the races but the most flamboyant in fashion. African Americans spend more than $50 billion on clothes and shoes.[12] We often define fashion. Designers from the fashion capitals of the world—New York, Paris, Milan, and Toyko—take their cues from us. We are their creative inspiration, yet we own only a few major factories or fashion lines. Often, we advertise for companies for free by wearing their logos on our caps, T-shirts, and gym shoes. Karl Kani Infinity and Terry Manufacturing are the only African American fashion lines to have made the big time. We have a long way to go.

Young African Americans are making strong statements with their clothes. Often, they are trying to blend in and impress their peers. Who would have thought that one day Stacey Adams would be replaced by Nike gym shoes? Here are some statements that they appear to be making:

1. I am bad.
2. I am rich.
3. I don't need you.
4. You owe me.
5. I don't have to respect you.

6. I don't have to work.
7. I only wear the best.
8. I am grown.
9. I owe you nothing.
10. I do what I want to do.
11. You can't tell me what to do.
12. I am promiscuous.
13. I am somebody.

Where do children get the money to pay for these clothes that are often highly inappropriate? Parents, please pay close attention to what your child is wearing and how he or she is wearing it. Extreme or unkempt ways of dressing are clues to the inner turmoil children are often experiencing.

African Americans, you know you are the Best Dressed, but in the great scheme of things, is that important? Why is it so important to make a statement with your style of dress? Why are you spending all your money to put on a front? Wake up! Let them make it and let them wear it themselves. Keep your money in your pocket.

Another question: How many of us are supporting struggling Black designers, clothing store owners, seamstresses, etc.? How many of us are so dependent on Whites to make and sell our clothes that we would be walking around naked without them?

Probably the only industry in which we support our own is in hair care, specifically, beauticians and barbers. Thanks to Madame C. J. Walker for starting that trend.

Since fashion is an industry that Blacks patronize, we should become major players in its production. Fashion is not the only way to make money in the garment industry. For example, *Black Enterprise* reports that Clotee McAfee, founder of Uniformity L.L.C., manufactures school uniforms. McAfee's uniforms are worn by more than 18,000 middle and high school students in New York, New Jersey, Texas, California, and Washington, DC.[13]

Since they get many of their fashions from you anyway, isn't it time to profit from your innate creativity and style? It's time to stop following the Calvin's, Liz's, and Donna's. Who are they to feed our style back to us *in season*? We will wear what we want to wear and when we want to wear it. Start sewing for yourself, and support your brothers and sisters in the fashion industry. This is how we'll become financially strong.

Merging Our Wealth

As African Americans enter into the 21st century, will we be the only group of people left without a slice of the American economic pie, either by design or through extreme negligence and selfishness on our part?

In 1997, Earl G. Graves Ltd., the parent of Black Enterprise magazine launched the Black Enterprise/ Greenwich Street Fund, a private equity investment vehicle, to finance black-owned companies with gross sales between $10 and $100 million. Carlton L. Guthrie, the CEO of Lansing, Michigan-based Trumark Inc., one of the nation's largest auto suppliers, took a different approach. Last year he teamed up with CEOs, bankers and corporate professionals to create the Runners Club, an advisory group focused on transforming small black businesses into BE's 100 companies. The BE 100s companies must take the lead in creating more large black-owned businesses,' asserts Guthrie. That's what we are trying to do with this program.[14]

African Americans like to flaunt their wealth. We envy our entertainers and sports celebrities who drive the fanciest cars and dress in the most expensive clothes. Yet, many do not give back to the communities that raised them, nourished them, and educated them. It is not okay to turn your back on your community. Before we were "given permission" to integrate with White people, we lived, worked, worshipped, and went to school with one another. The rich and the poor lived side by side. We employed our own. We didn't even have the phrase "give back to the community" because we naturally supported each other. This is the spirit we must reclaim if we are to survive and thrive in the new millennium.

Every day in the business press, we hear of some new corporate entity being created by the merger of companies. If corporations can come together, why can't we?

African American wealth will grow through the processes of duplication and unification. Wealthy African Americans must find ways to duplicate themselves, whether through education, mentorship, providing seed money, or contributing funds to an educational institution, like Bill and Camile Cosby did for Spelman College. Unification will occur with mergers, alliances, and partnerships. We've got to stop being mistrustful of each other. The time is now to come together!

As Maulana Karenga has said,

> Undoubtedly the most important resource structure in solving Black problems is the Black community itself. Regardless of external goodwill, a people must initiate and lead the struggle for its own liberation. However, this necessitates the structural capacity—an institutional and organizational network—to wage such a struggle.[15]

We are the only race that lacks a structured economic base. We must create one within our own ranks first before we can think of merging and doing business with other communities.

Wealth Building Begins with You

Think of the poverty that exists in the African American community as temporary. Think of your own financial struggles as temporary. According to the Census Bureau, African American poverty rates dropped (from 33.1 percent to 30.6 percent).[16] The number of poor African Americans dipped from 9.7 million in 1996 to 9.1 million in 1997. Some of us are climbing out. Success is contagious. As the number of successful, wealthy African Americans grows, our community will become prosperous and strong.

With hard work and perseverance, you can remove yourself from poverty. When you do, remember to always keep your wealth circulating in your community by supporting Black businesses.

Manage Debt

Last but not least, it is critical that African Americans and their families get out of the debt trap. It is just another form of slavery. Could our high debt be causing our high rates of hypertension? Because of our love of high cost prestige items, we let ourselves get talked into buying furniture, clothes, cars, etc. that cost way beyond our means.

According to the Federal Reserve Board's Survey of Consumer Finances (SCF), most families (75 percent) had some type of debt (including mortgage debt) in 1995.[17]

Some financial planners believe that leveraging debt to build wealth is a wise strategy. But I believe, "never a borrower or a lender be." Common sense says that it's time to stop accumulating debt in amounts greater than your ability to pay. If your debt is more than 25 percent of your income, you're probably struggling.

It is very difficult to fix your credit report if you get in trouble. Credit abuse places an extreme burden on individuals, couples, and families. They can send an individual back to square one time and again. However, with some planning and discipline, we can begin to restore our financial health and patch up the money leaks in our multibillion dollar wealth.

REASON 3—LACK OF EDUCATION

There is no excuse for African Americans to not enjoy a higher level of educational achievement. We have access to free public education and there are many movements to put education back into the hands of parents. It is up to us to take control of our schools. Here are six educational goals to drive our efforts into the next millennium:

1. To provide educational opportunities for every African American from the cradle to the grave.
2. To produce at least one African American scientist per state for the next 30 years.
3. To produce at least one African American doctor per state for the next 30 years.
4. To give our full attention to developing and implementing African-centered early education teaching methods and curricula that are infused with an understanding of childhood developmental stages, love, understanding, and compassion.
5. To mandate that African American educators refrain from promiscuous and other inappropriate activities with students.
6. to assist deserving African American college-bound students.

Keep these goals in mind as you read the rest of this chapter.

History of African American Education

Wesley and other African American scholars have described the thirst for knowledge our forefathers and mothers had at the end of the 19th century and at the turn of the 20th. Having been denied the right to an education during slavery, we went after our education with a vengeance. Wesley says that the illiteracy rate among African Americans fell from 81 percent in 1870 to 57 percent in 1890.[1]

Today, African Americans and Hispanics have the highest illiteracy rates in the country. What has happened to our zeal for education? Surely times were much more difficult for Africans during the Reconstruction years, yet they were determined to get the education that had been denied them during slavery. Today, we can get it free, but do not want it.

Illiteracy can lead to poverty, crime (inmates are often illiterate), powerlessness, and low self-worth. People who are illiterate cannot read a street sign, enjoy the beauty of a Walter Mosely novel, fill out a job application, or balance a checkbook. Illiteracy lowers the quality of life. The good news is, illiteracy can be remedied. There are many worthwhile programs that are committed to raising the literacy rates of African American adults and children. The schools that most often succeed at raising and consistently achieving high reading scores are committed to an interdisciplinary style of teaching, in which all faculty and staff, from the math teacher to the gym teacher to the English teacher, teach reading.

One thing is for certain. You can't get a degree if you can't read. By 1892, Blacks had earned 3,700 college degrees.[2] According to the US Census, in 1998, 86 percent of African American adults aged 25-29 and over had a high school diploma, compared to 51 percent in 1980.[3] We're doing better, but our goal should be 100 percent!

Learning should not stop just because you've received your high school diploma or college degree. For African Americans to succeed in life we must be committed to life long learning.

As the United Negro College Fund motto says, "A mind is a terrible thing to waste." A mind is also a terrible thing to leave home without, but that is just what you're doing when you refuse to visit a library, drop out of school, do not read to your children, and do not read a book yourself. The path to financial prosperity is paved with education. Likewise, the path to poverty is paved with ignorance and illiteracy.

Just as we must have a financial plan for ourselves and our families, we must have an educational plan for ourselves and our children. That includes developing a plan for financing tuition, fees, room, and board—whether at a historically Black college, major university, or trade school. From the time they are in the womb, plan and save toward your children's education. Talk to your child constantly about college. One mother buys her children T-shirts from many colleges. This is a much more empowering fashion statement than wearing clothes with checks and sports logos. Take family trips to college campuses. If colleges in your area provide summer camps, send your children if you can afford to do so. Tell them stories about family members who went to and graduated from college. Keep your expectations high, and your children will try and meet them.

Historically Black Colleges
According to Dr. Stephen J. Wright, former president of Fisk University,

> Although called "colleges and universities", he maintains, "these institutions were little more than elementary and high schools," since qualified preparatory schools were totally lacking. Though the Morrill Act of 1890 opened many tax-supported land grant colleges, the southern states failed to maintain the black schools in accord with the separate but equal doctrine, and their major problem became that of merely surviving. That 115 Negro Colleges have survived despite handicaps is largely owing to private philanthropy.[4]
>
> A group of Carnegie Foundation Researchers, headed by Professor Earl McGrath, reported

in 1965 that many of the predominantly Negro Colleges could eliminate or at least mitigate their present shortcomings and needs if they had additional financial resources. Nearly half of the Negro College presidents interviewed by McGrath pinpointed their financial condition as the most crucial weakness in their institutions.[5]

Every graduate from a historically Black college (HBC) must come out of hiding and tell his or her story to a child or young person trying to decide where to go to school. HBCs are the best known secrets in higher education. They provide a safe haven for African American students to learn and grow as mature individuals. Where mainstream universities seldom give us the attention academically we may need or deserve, HBCs are there, teaching, admonishing, and nurturing. HBCs have a tremendous success rate in graduating many of our leading doctors, engineers, educators, writers, and thinkers. HBC alumni are part of a great legacy of African American education. Not only should we be proud, we should sing our story to anyone who will listen. All African Americans, whether a HBC alumnus or not, should contribute financially to Black colleges.

Not many of us can contribute as much money as Bill Cosby, and that is not necessary. Just give what you can from the heart. My challenge to HBC graduates is to contribute $1.00 per week for the rest of their lives as a "thank you" gesture to their alma mater. Think of it as an investment. If just 100,000 HBC graduates would commit to this nominal contribution, we could wipe out ignorance, illiteracy, and poverty in our community.

HBC administrators must hold themselves accountable for every penny donated. Our contributions to your schools are a sacred trust. We are depending on you to make good use of this money by hiring the best professors and developing the best programs for our young people.

REASON 4—LACK OF DISCIPLINE

Remember the saying, "Spare the rod, spoil the children?" The rod was not about beating children, but was a symbol of the discipline parents must instill in their children. We live in an era in which we have lost control of our children. We've lost the ability, and the will, to tell our children what to do, how to do it, and when to do it. Author Jawanza Kunjufu believes that the problem can be directly traced to our change in values and the influence of television. "I believe children want to be disciplined, they want to know someone cares about them, they want a leader, they want to be corrected so they can learn rules and codes of behavior so eventually—not immediately—they can become leaders."[1]

We must reclaim our children, and we must do it now. We are in a crisis that threatens the survival of future generations. Control begins at home first, and then spreads out into our schools and communities. Parents, whether married or single, cannot continue to delegate the raising and disciplining of their children to relatives, teachers, and other caretakers. Parenting is a full-time responsibility. Our children are out of control because we have relinquished our responsibility to TV, peers, and others. I am appalled to see young children who have the run of stores with the apparent blessing of the parent. African American parents must learn to tell their children, "Stop! Don't do that! Leave it alone! Sit down! Be quiet! Come here! Don't talk, listen!" And above all you've got to *mean it*. These commands must be given firmly, fairly, and with love. Our parents were strict disciplinarians. Why we can't discipline our children is beyond me. We can't blame it on hard times; we have always had difficulties. In fact, during the Reconstruction and Jim Crow years, times were much more difficult. There are elders still alive today who witnessed lynchings and maybe even barely escaped danger themselves at the hands of White people.

Maybe we just don't understand what it means to be free. We think that being free means that we can do whatever we want. For example, we can have irresponsible sex, but not raise the children that are produced from the act. Our children are growing up with the wrong idea about freedom, and as their primary teachers, they're learning it from us. Freedom has a price and a responsibility. Freedom is not free.

Some parents had such difficult childhoods that they have vowed to make life easier for their children. They say, "I am just trying to give my children some of the things I didn't have." The parent has to work long hours to make this easy childhood happen. As a result, parents are away from the home more than they are at home. This has created an entire generation of African American "latchkey kids," spoiled with material goods and lacking in discipline. Like Dr. Kunjufu says, spending time with your children is more important than buying them stuff that will just break anyway. Stop right now. Your parents didn't give you everything you wanted and you turned out okay. Don't give them another thing. Instead, give them your time and love. Teach them to obey their elders and to be decent citizens. Teach them morals, virtues, spirituality, love, and decency. Learn to say "no" with love and understanding. For the material goods your children want (not need), let them earn the money to buy it themselves.

Train your child in the way they should go and when they grow older they will not depart from your training. That's biblical, and no truer words were ever written. How many of us today can still remember one particular time when a parent had to discipline? We may joke about it now, but thank God they had the strength to make us see the error of our ways. They were not trying to be our friends. They were being good parents. If tough love is necessary, use it. Draw a line in the sand. If your child steps over the line, dish out fair, tough, and reasonable punishment. Make a tough love decision and stick to it. You will not regret it!

Sometimes I get embarrassed for the parents of children who have no self-control. Many feel exhausted and powerless. Still, they are your children. You brought them into the world, and they are your responsibility. Save yourself a lot of trouble and embarrassment by training them at home. Let them know who is in control. Establish rules for behavior in the home and in public. Let your children know what the cost will be for breaking the rules, and if they do, don't talk, take action. Lay the groundwork from the moment your child is born. There's been a lot of talk about child abuse, but if the parent is truly disciplining the child out of a healthy love, there will be no abusive behavior. Even while you are disciplining your children, let them know that you love them. Instilling love and discipline from infancy will help prevent an out-of-control life, one filled with drugs, teen pregnancy, and violence.

REASON 5—WELFARE

What is the real purpose of welfare? What was it designed for? Was it set up to help people who needed help? Or was it designed to control and "herd" Black people? Has this program been beneficial to African Americans?

The most devastating effect of welfare was how it helped to dismantle the Black family. Support would go to the female head of household based on the number of dependents she had. As long as no man was present in the home, the welfare system would pay the mother for her dependents. With a male presence, however, payments were either terminated or reduced. The welfare system appears to have been designed to keep the male out of the home at all cost. It was never designed to make a family strong or unified.

Was the welfare system deliberately designed to keep the African American male out of the household? Perhaps we'll never have hard proof, but we can observe the results. Welfare created a culture in which African American males believed that it was okay to jump from one female to another, making babies, and trusting in the system to take care of them. I believe that while welfare was promoted as a way to help families in crisis, the true purpose was to destroy African American families. If the goal had been to keep families together, then checks would have been disbursed whether or not the father was still at home. How many Black families would be together today had the laws been written to more noble ends?

Yet, welfare served a useful purpose. As Romans 8:28 says, "All things work together for good to them that love the Lord and are called according to His purpose." Thanks to the media, we know about all of the negative, isolated incidents of mothers who sent their daughters out to conceive babies just to increase their welfare checks or the lady who adopted 18 anonymous children to increase her food stamp allotment. These cases are the exceptions to the rule. Overall, welfare has res--cued many families in crisis. For many people, welfare was their only means of support.

On August 22, 1996, welfare as we knew it ceased to exist when President Clinton signed the Personal Responsibility and Work Opportunity Reconciliation Act (P.L. 104-193). In January 1997, Congress initiated a new "Right to Work Initiative," which finished the job.[1]

Teenagers, control your sexual desires because welfare as we knew it is gone forever. Your first baby will be your last taste of freedom!

REASON 6—TEEN PREGNANCY

Is it morally right to give birth control to teenagers? Has giving birth control to teenagers helped to eliminate teen pregnancy and sexually transmitted diseases? What mixed messages are we giving teenagers by giving them condoms and birth control pills?

In his book *How to Help Your Child Thrive and Survive in Public School,* Cliff Schimmels provides an interesting analysis of the challenges facing teens today. He says that "Nature and culture join forces in a conspiracy against adolescents. Nature equips them with the desires and functions of human sexuality. Culture restricts their use of those functions . . . Many don't survive the conflict."[1]

I am worried about the future of young people and the future of our race. If children continue to have children, we will not survive. Parents, teachers, ministers, and all adults who love our young people, make a copy of the following letter and give it to every female teen you know.

Dear Young Lady,

In this letter I'm going to give you the truth from a man's point of view. I've written this letter because so many young females your age are having sex and getting pregnant. It occurred to me that maybe you might not understand how a woman gets pregnant and what it means to be a teen mother. A female gets pregnant when she has sexual intercourse with a male without any form of birth control. Some girls don't believe that you can get pregnant the first time or if a boy withdraws from you, but it's true. You can get pregnant the first time you have sex, and you can get pregnant even if your partner withdraws from you during the sex act.

If you're thinking about having sex, or are being pressured into having sex, think about what it would be like to be a mother. Your baby would be helpless and totally dependent on you. Most teen mothers raise their babies alone because the father usually leaves. Even nice guys might not stick around. Sometimes grandmother might be able to help with babysitting, but is that fair to her? No, it's not, because she's already got her hands full trying to take care of you.

When a teenager gets pregnant, she gives up her freedom. Remember hanging out with your friends? Going to parties? Dating? Planning for the future? All those pleasant things would be gone. You'd never seem to have enough money. Some teen mothers have to drop out of school to try and find work. And forget about welfare. The government is getting rid of it even as you're reading these words.

Keep your precious freedom while you are young. Keep control of your life and your future by not having sex. Stay a virgin. If you've already had sex, practice abstinence. It's never too late to begin saying no. Wait until you're married to a man who genuinely loves you and who is ready to take care of you and a family. Smart teens around the country are beginning to get the message. Having sex at your age is not worth the risk. Especially for females. Why? It is because you have the most to lose. If you get pregnant, you're the one who would have to take care of the baby. It's not fair, but that's just how it is.

Females are at a higher risk of getting a sexually transmitted disease than males. You've been taught safe sex, but the safest sex is abstinence. So often girls are convinced to have sex without any form of protection. This is dangerous. Better to let the guy go. In this day and age, any guy who would insist on having sex with no protection is selfish and not worth your time. He's not concerned with your health or your future, only his needs.

If a female has sex without the protection of marriage, she is not respected by males. Stay a virgin until you're married. I know there is a lot of pressure to have sex, but be strong. Your body is your own. Don't believe anybody who says, "If you loved me, you'd make love to me." That's a lie. The truth is, if he loved you, he wouldn't pressure you to have sex. He wouldn't put your future at risk. He'd cherish you.

The power to say no is within you, so play it smart. Don't put yourself in any compromising positions when you're with a guy. Do not go into his home when no adult is there. Don't get into heavy petting. Don't speak intimacies late into the night on the phone. If you must talk about such things, talk to him in the presence of your parents.

Never compromise your morals and values. Practice being the decent young lady that you are. Watch what you wear. You can be fashionable and decent at the same time. Watch your language. Watch how you dance. Pay attention to the words of your favorite songs. Some of them are not fit to be heard by anyone, much less someone your age. Be feminine, smart, and dignified. If you respect yourself at all times, males will have no choice but to respect you too.

Your chastity, intelligence, and freedom are the most precious assets you own. Keep your undergarments up, your dress down, and your legs crossed tightly together. This formula worked for the women of generations past, and it will work for you today.

Make a male work for you, because you are a treasure of great value. He will not value you if you make it too easy on him. If you chase after him, you demean your value in his eyes. If you go slow, you will discover in your own time whether you really like the guy or not.

Don't buy expensive and fancy gifts for him. Don't be so available when he calls. If you have a full life, you won't be sitting by the phone—so go and get a good life. If a guy wants to date you and he asks you out on a date, he should pay. That means no "dutch" dates, where you pay for your ticket and he pays for his. If he doesn't have enough money, he shouldn't be asking you out.

If the guy begins to pressure you to have sex, consider this a big red flag, and get out of the relationship. Even if it hurts. Better your heart now than your mind, body, soul, and pocketbook for the rest of your life.

There is nothing wrong with being wooed and pursued but never allow yourself to be subdued. Do not make the mistake of substituting sex for love—there is a difference. Yours truly,

Jimmy

A major reason why teen pregnancy exists is because teens have too much unsupervised time after school. From the end of 10th period to the arrival home of the parent(s) from work, a danger zone exists during which teens get together to have sex, do drugs, and in general get in trouble. Schimmels recommends afterschool programs with adult supervision. "There are several reasons why Christian students and parents should consider active and consistent participation in some school-sponsored, extracurricular program. These programs can provide a benefit both to the student and to the parent and can help get maximum value from the public school experience."[2]

There is a light at the end of the tunnel, and parents and teenagers should be encouraged. Studies on teen sexual behavior are revealing that teen sexual activity is on the decline.

Dr. Martin Luther King, Jr. gave this advice to a young lady who had experienced pregnancy out of wedlock. She and the father got married, and he constantly reminded her of it. As a result, the marriage failed. What should she do to atone for her mistake? Dr. King said,

> Your problem is one that must find its solution in the domains of psychology and religion. There is the danger that you will develop a morbid sense of guilt as well as an extremely sensitive attitude toward your past mistake. This would be tragic. You must somehow turn your vision toward the future rather than the past. You should concentrate on the heights which you are determined to reach, not look back into the depth which you once fell. With this wholesome attitude you will be able to stand up amid all of the criticisms that persons in your town will direct toward you. In other words, you can so outlive your past mistake that even the most ardent critic will develop a warm respect for you. You can still live in the same town and win the respect of the community. I would also suggest that you give your life to certain high and noble pursuits. In so doing, you will be able to concentrate on such challenging and ennobling ideas that you will not have the time for self-pity.[3]

All of us make mistakes, but not all of us learn from them. If you know a teen who is pregnant, being pressured into having sex, or has contracted a sexually transmitted disease, give her hope. Yes, life will be much more difficult, but we have a history of overcoming adversity. Tell her that she too can overcome, but the first step is to learn from her mistakes and to not repeat them.

Parents and caretakers, you can never spend too much quality time with your children. Talk to them and listen to them. Don't let yourself get so busy that you lose your child forever.

Reason 7—Drugs

Drug use and drug dealing continue to wreak havoc in the African American community. It has been said that only crack cocaine could cause a Black mother to abuse and neglect her child. Were these drugs designed just for us—to keep us controlled or to kill us off? The CIA may have been responsible for bringing drugs into our neighborhoods, but no one forced any of us to shoot, sniff, or sell drugs.

I designed the following survey to get you thinking about your feelings and experiences with drugs. Get out a pencil and sheet of paper and answer the following questions honestly and at length. No one will see your answers but you.

1. Are illegal drugs beneficial in any way?
2. Have you ever thought that drugs could help you (or Black people) in some way?
3. Who brought drugs to your attention?
4. Why were drugs brought to your attention?
5. Are drug prevention efforts effective in keeping African American youth drug-free?
6. Why are Black people selling illegal drugs? Is money the only reason?
7. Were Black people hand picked to sell drugs?
8. Where do illegal drugs come from?
9. Who sets the price and dosage of illegal drugs?
10. Are African Americans being used as guinea pigs to test the effects of illegal drugs on body, mind, and soul?
11. When does it become okay to kill for drugs?
12. Are illegal drugs really addictive?
13. Can illegal drugs make you an addict for life?

14. Is it possible to fully recover from a drug addiction?
15. Can you quit whenever you want?
16. Does crime pay?

    The sale and abuse of illegal drugs are wreaking havoc in the African American community. Since the average Black person on the street does not have the money to finance the large scale purchase, importation, and distribution of drugs, we can assume that others outside our community are behind the drug trade. That does not excuse our participation, but to remedy the problem, we have to understand the big picture.

    Some Black people have so little faith in God's ability to provide that they have turned to selling drugs as a way of creating wealth and prestige. An entire underground culture has sprung up as a result. Unfortunately, our young people are the greatest victims. Lured by the promise of easy money and escape from the day-to-day difficulties of life, they sell drugs and use drugs. Too many Black youth are dying at a young age. The following warning signs have been provided by the National Drug Control Policy in Washington, D.C. They indicate whether a young person may be having a problem with drugs:

1.   Drop in academic performance.
2.   Lack of interest in personal appearance.
3.   Withdrawal, isolation, depression, fatigue.
4.   Aggressive, rebellious behavior.
5.   Hostility and lack of cooperativeness.
6.   Deteriorating relationships with family.
7.   Change in friends.
8.   Loss of interest in hobbies and/or sports.
9.   Change in eating/sleeping habits.
10. Evidence of drugs or drug paraphernalia (e.g., needles, pipes, papers, lighters).
11. Physical changes (e.g., runny noses not from cold, red eyes, coughing, wheezing, bruises, needle marks).[1]

If you've noticed any of these signs, get help for your child right away before it's too late. We must do everything we can to help our children and young people stay drug free. Help is available. For more information call 800/666-3332 and ask for the *Drug Free Parents Guide*. In case of an emergency, call the following hotline numbers: 800/662-HELP or 800/821-HELP.

Innovative Solutions

We must teach our youth that building wealth legally is not only possible, it is the only way. But first, we must get drugs out of ourselves, families, neighborhoods, churches, and schools.

Create legal drugs. Instead of selling illegal drugs to one another, killing one another for the sake of a dollar, why not develop legal drugs from the herbs of the earth to help heal the world? If Eli Lilly can make billions manufacturing drugs of questionable benefit, surely we can reclaim our African heritage of healing mind, body, and soul by researching, manufacturing, and marketing medicinals.

Make and sell legal products. Using the same entrepreneurial and marketing skills that it takes to sell illegal drugs, create a new, legal product to sell that will benefit our community and create wealth for you and your family. If African Americans can convince others to use something that will kill them, it would not be difficult to sell them a product that will enhance their life and positively meet their needs.

Get rehabilitated. Those of you who are currently using, do yourself, your family, and the entire Black community a favor and enroll into a rehab program. Make it your goal to never use drugs again.

Get off drugs for your baby's sake. Pregnant mothers, you are carrying life inside of your bodies. Your baby is a gift from God. Is not this gift more worthy than your pipe or syringe? *You* are a gift from God. Get off drugs for yourself and your baby. Give health, not death. Don't subject your baby to life as a newborn drug addict. Let me ask you this: do you want your child to lead the same kind of life you are now leading? One that involves robbing, lying, prostituting, killing, and cheating? Do you want them to struggle in school with Attention Deficit Disorder? Do you want them to have no self-respect? What about AIDS? If you're shooting, you could catch AIDS and pass it on to your innocent baby. My prayer is that you will drug no more!

Boycott Hollywood. Hollywood has desensitized us to crime by glamorizing drugs, violence, and gangs. Young people have a difficult time understanding that bullets really do hurt. Drugs really can kill. Actors and actresses who star in these movies do not die on the set, but in real life, people die of criminal activity every day. When are you going to wake up and stop believing the lie that Hollywood has sold you? We do not need the fantasy. We're strong. We can deal with the truth. We can use our minds and the power of faith to solve any problem.

The Black church must take a stand. Gregory Reed says that "though a solution to the dilemma may seem far off, churches can help in solving the problem. Church-based drug treatment and counseling programs can be used to help those who cannot get help elsewhere. Proper planning and organization can make the establishing of either program possible. Once this has been done, then it can begin creating a program to satisfy the needs of its community."[2]

We Must Survive!

The cycle of drug selling, drug use, and drug addiction is ongoing and ugly. It never gets better. The current drug scene in African American neighborhoods has created living conditions comparable to an outbreak of bubonic plague. If we don't eliminate this negative element, we will surely die. How can we accomplish anything of value if we are high on drugs or sitting in a jail cell because we got caught selling drugs? Black people, leave the drugs alone. Don't even get started using or selling them. Education, love, and unity are the tickets to empowerment, not an illegal, deadly substance.

REASON 8—LACK OF MORALS

When it comes to morals, we lack a healthy respect for the principles of right and wrong. The African American race has reached an all time low in doing what is morally right and an all time high in doing what is morally wrong. We have lost respect for our elders, babies, children, peers, parents, neighborhoods, and above all ourselves.

Is TV the cause of our moral decay? Is it greed? Will we do anything, including lie, cheat, and steal, just to be accepted as a member of the "in" crowd? Is it because our children are raising themselves while we, their parents and caretakers, are busy running the streets? Somehow we must find a way to raise the standards in our behavior toward one another.

We are so much like the biblical children of Israel. Having spent years wandering in the wilderness, they too lost their morals and allegiance to God. So God gave Moses 10 laws to control their behavior. They were:

1.   You may worship no other God than me.
2.   You shall not make yourselves any idols: No images of animals, birds, or fish.
3.   You shall not use the name of Jehovah your God irreverently, nor use it to swear to a falsehood.
4.   Remember to observe the Sabbath as a holy day.
5.   Honor you father and your mother, that you may have a long, good life in the land the Lord your God will give you.
6.   You must not murder.
7.   You must not commit adultery.

8. You must not steal.
9. You must not lie.
10. You must not be envious of your neighbor's house, or want to sleep with his wife, or want to own his slaves, oxen, donkeys, or anything else he has.[1]

Nowhere in my Bible does God say that the 10 Commandments were for the Israelites only. They are for us too, and we are in desperate need of their guidance and wisdom. Following the 10 Commandments is the first step toward gaining respect for ourselves and others and learning how to treat people right.

Recently, Congress discussed the idea of mandating that the 10 Commandments be posted in every classroom in America. I'd go one step further. The 10 Commandments should be posted in the White House (especially the Oval Office), the Pentagon, along the walls of the Congressional Assembly, and every church, police station, courthouse, penitentiary, grocery store, and home in America. Children have learned from us how to break the 10 Commandments, so they must learn from us how to follow them.

R - E - S - P - E - C - T !

Aretha Franklin sang her heart out about respect back in the '60s, and we still haven't figured it out. Respect is earned and not given. You must respect yourself and others, then and only then will you receive respect in return. Forget the brother who stepped on your gymshoes or accidentally bumped against you. That's not *dis*respectful. That was probably an accident. Respect yourself and respect your brother too!

The mandate to respect ourselves and others comes after the 10 Commandments. This will help instill a stronger sense of African values in our behaviors and thoughts. Like Spike Lee said, let's all "do the right thing."

Strategies for Dealing with Immorality

Beware of people who compliment you too much. They may not mean it. In fact, they may mean you harm. Black people have become very jealous of one another's success. They may just be lulling you into a false sense of security so that they can rob you blind.

Doctors must heal body, mind, and soul. Today's African American doctors must reclaim the African way of healing. The African-centered style of healing involves not only treating the body, but the moral fiber of the person. If your morals are high but your behaviors are low life, this will create confusion in your soul and sickness in your body.

Doctors too must be held to a strict standard of morality. They have an honored position in our culture, and that trust is not to be betrayed. They must not abuse their authority. They must not succumb to lustful temptations with patients or any other unethical practices.

Stop stealing. Stop killing. While a prisoner in Rome, Paul told the church at Asia Minor to live right. He said, "If anyone is stealing he must stop it and begin using those hands of his for honest work so he can give to others in need."[2]

According to Charles Wesley, our slave ancestors were sometimes guilty of stealing.

Where the slaves food supply was inadequate and there was a plentiful supply in the storehouse, kitchen or field, the habit of pilfering and foraging for food readily developed. As a result of this situation, it was asserted that the habit of stealing was a fixed trait of Negro slaves. When such habits developed, they were, of course, the result of the conditions slaves were forced to live under rather than an indication of racial proclivities.[3]

43

Have you ever been a robbery victim? Nine times out of ten, the thief is someone you know. He or she may live in your home or down the street. He may be your child's friend or your cousin's boyfriend. People who steal have no intention of ever getting a job. They feel the world and you owe them something, and that's why they feel justified in stealing from you.

It is because of the thieves in our midst that our homes are caged in with wrought iron doors, bars on the windows, and alarm systems. The thief has become so bold that he will wait for you to come home so that he can rob and kill you.

The challenge to African Americans and the rest of the world is to stop the stealing and killing. We must remove these shackles of the devil from our feet. When asked, "How can the crime wave among Negroes be reduced?" Dr. King said,

There is both an external and internal solution to this problem. Both must work simultaneously if the problem is to be solved. The external solution to the problem is to work passionately and unrelentingly to remove the conditions which make crime possible. The Negro is not criminal by nature. Indeed, criminality is environmental, not racial. Poverty and ignorance breed crime whatever the racial group may be. So we must work to remove the system of segregation, discrimination, and the existence of economic injustice if we are to solve the problem of crime in the Negro community. For these external factors are casually responsible for crime. On the other hand, the Negro must work within the community to solve the problem while the external cause factors are being removed.[4]

Be honest. Webster defines integrity as "adherence to a code of morals; the quality or state of being complete or undivided." When we say one thing then do another, we are divided, incomplete. Without honesty and integrity, we will never unify as a race because we'll never be able to trust one another.

We are guilty of not keeping our word or commitment on the smallest of projects. In your church, local schools, and community, there are probably just a few dedicated people who do all the volunteer work. Everyone else makes promises and then fails to come through. This is dishonest behavior and it makes us weak. If you can't work on a project, be honest. State up front that you cannot or will not work.

African Americans must stop lying to each other. Be a man or woman of your word. There was a time in our not too distant past when there were no written contracts among us. We trusted each other enough to shake hands on a deal. Integrity was everything. If you didn't keep up your end of the deal, your reputation would be spread throughout the community as one who could not be trusted. Our word was our bond. We didn't need a paper contract to make us act right. Like Dennis Kimbro says, "Integrity develops a sound and dependable character. It also attracts others who believe in this trait. Practicing integrity provides you with a feeling of self-reliance and self-respect, and gives a clear conscience."[5]

The Ultimate Commandment

Jesus made some very definitive statements in the Bible about love that bear directly on our need to seed our moral ground. We must replace the lying, cheating, stealing, robbing, and killing with the following seven commandments of love.

1. Love yourself first and foremost.
2. Love your neighbor just as you love yourself.
3. Love and honor your father and mother.
4. Love your sisters and brothers.

5. Love your spouse and children.
6. Love everyone, including animals and all of nature.
7. Love God Almighty as He continues to love you.

Love is the most powerful force in the universe. With love, we can make a difference. We can rehabilitate our people. With love, criminals can become productive citizens.

To love is to care about your neighbor. When was the last time you checked on the elder down the street? Is she eating? Does he have heat? When you see young people doing well, give them praise. If they're making trouble, admonish them—whether they're your children or not. We are each other's keeper.

In August 1963, African Americans marched in unity to Washington, D.C. On October 16, 1995, more than one million African American men marched peacefully to Washington. Apart from those two times, excluding sporting events, when was the last time we came together? The commitments made by Dr. King and Minister Farrakhan provided models of responsibility that we must all emulate. We don't have to wait for a well-known recognized leader to unify us. You can begin in your family, on your block, in your school and church. This is the only way we'll kill the cancer that destroys us from within.

Lay down your egos, bitterness, and pride. Respect and love one another. Care about your brothers and sisters. Commit yourself to helping lift up all African Americans.

REASON 9—THE JINX OF SLAVERY

One of the negative stereotypes of African Americans is that we are lazy. But tell me, who is lazy? The one who works like an animal in the field or the one who forces others to work for him?

To turn an African into a slave, the White slave owners resorted to methods that dehumanized and subdued us. Many scholars have told of the horrific conditions aboard the slave ships, where our ancestors were packed into the ships with virtually no space between them, shackled at the ankles. The lack of sanitation created a breeding ground for diseases. And on the plantation, the horrors did not end. Our ancestors were beaten, starved, raped, and worked literally to death.

Are we still suffering the effects of slavery today? Does the slave mindset still exist today?

Those of us who understand what happened to our ancestors are striving to eliminate the slavery mindset from our own consciousness. There are still millions of us, however, who do not know or care about what happened in the past. If you don't know your history, you're bound to repeat it. African-centered education is the cure for a slave mentality, but because we are in denial about our past, we are repeating it. Because we are not teaching our children, the slave mentality has been reborn in them.

We were jinxed by 400 years of servitude. Webster defines a jinx as "a condition or spell of misfortune." Slavery was the condition that produced our misfortune and the effects linger with us today.

We have not moved farther along as a race because we are still in denial about slavery. If you try and solve your problems without taking slavery into consideration, you are doomed to failure. We are like the young elephant that is tied to a stake in the ground. Because the rope is short, the elephant can only move a short distance. He struggles to pull up the stake, but to no avail. So he circles around the stake and soon he becomes comfortable with his little territory. After a while, the elephant's obedience is tested. The rope is removed and the trainer watches to see just how far away from the stake the elephant will move. If he stays close to the stake, he is considered obedient and well trained. If not, more work needs to be done.

The elephant's obedience was not inherited. It was not natural to him. He became obedient because the trainer forced the animal into a controlled environment that was specifically designed to change his behavior.

Our ancestors were treated like the elephant. We were tied to a stake and threatened with death if we dared to move beyond a circumscribed area of thought, speech, and action. Africans were not born slaves. Rather, a passive, obedient mentality had to be created within us.

On January 1, 1863, our bodies walked away from the plantations, but our minds stayed. We never received the healing that we so desperately needed. As a result, our ancestors passed down those behaviors and attitudes that made them slaves to us today. Yes, we are still bound by a slave mentality.

Do we want out of that circle? Are we willing to pay the price to be re-educated and healed? On the plantation, many insidious strategies were used to divide us to prevent insurrections. The worse was division based on skin complexion. The darker Africans worked the fields, the lighter ones worked in the big house. Today, skin color and hair texture still divide us. Brothers and sisters, it doesn't matter where you work on the plantation, you are all slaves!

According to our definition of a jinx, we can agree that Whites created a condition of misfortune. However, that does not mean that we can't break the spell. We can and we must.

Our minds are powerful. Today we can choose to not be spellbound. We can go after our healing. We can choose to be free.

The Bible says, "Fret not thyself because of evil doers, neither be thou envious against the workers of iniquity. For they shall soon be cut down like the grass, and wither as the green herb."[1] Take heart: What goes around comes around. In the meantime, we can't sit on our bitterness and anger. We must stand up and take our minds back. We must follow the example of those who have freed themselves. Dennis Kimbro says that "There is nothing in the universe that limits you, or that could or would desire to limit you. As long as you think you are inhibited, you will never rise above those boundaries."[2]

Reparations!

How will the nations of the world atone for the great sin of slavery? Welfare is not good enough. In fact, it was just a different type of slavery.

We never did get our 40 acres and a mule, and a promise is a promise. Since so many nations were involved in the slave trade, maybe the International Monetary Fund should fund our reparations. Amnesty International, the American Civil Liberties Union, the United Nations, and other international bodies should be involved in correcting this ancient injustice against us. Without reparations and the request for forgiveness that is implied, there will never be peace among the races.

We have many qualified African American attorneys who could fight the good fight: Johnny Cochran, Willie Gary, John Wesley Brooks, Phillip Ragan, and Jenice Gholson-Dunlap, to name a few. All our great freedom fighters should come together and file one mega class action lawsuit against the perpetrating countries that participated in the capture, transportation, and enslavement of Africans who were forced to become slaves.

In the meantime, we cannot wait on reparations to take charge of our communities and heal ourselves. Reeducating ourselves about our history is one way to heal. The following initiatives will heal us and build our community. We must . . .

1. Establish an African American Interdenominational Education Fund.
2. Establish manufacturing facilities that make every product we use.
3. Improve African American neighborhoods and schools and return to them in mass.
4. Remove illegal drugs from our neighborhoods.
5. Love our neighbors as we love ourselves.
6. Earnestly seek God in everything we do.

We are not a cursed people. No jinx has power over us if we come together. Let us walk off the plantation—body, mind, and soul—together. Let us seal the rifts that have separated us. As a healed, unified people, we can create jobs, live in nice homes, drive nice cars, wear nice clothes. We can raise our young people to become strong, productive adults. We've suffered enough. Let us go forward into a wonderful tomorrow.

REASON 10—THE CRISIS BETWEEN AFRICAN AMERICAN MEN AND WOMEN

Since the official end of slavery, the Black man has been systematically targeted for destruction. The most important part of that plan involves the Black woman. The African American female holds the key to reuniting and solidifying our families. It is through her that all of us were born. She is our first teacher, healer, and preacher. Thus, as the morals, thoughts, health, spirituality, and actions of the African American woman go, so does the nation.

Black women are not the cause of all the problems that face Black people. She has been victimized just as Black men. The difference between Black men and women, however, is that men know we've been victimized. Black women do not. Are African American females willing pawns in the conspiracy to destroy our love relationships and the African American family? Will they stay with African American men or abandon them? These questions must be addressed by our race. As African American women climb the corporate and economic ladders of success, they have been led to believe that. . .

1. They have no African male peers.
2. There is no conspiracy to separate her from African men.
3. They don't have to be strong. They don't have to hold our families together like their mothers and grandmothers did when the African male was under siege.

4. Their careers are more important than staying home and raising a family.
5. They do not have to sacrifice their "freedom" to unify our community and heal the Black family.
6. They are exempt from the problems and challenges facing African Americans.
7. They have an equal chance at success in corporate America.
8. They can engage in sexual promiscuity with no consequences.

Black women, you've been placed in corporate America for a reason: to make a difference in the lives of the African American family. Educated women, you have the ability and opportunity to create a massive change in the mindset of America. You hold the key to redefining affirmative action so that this policy will truly support and uplift our people. Like the biblical Queen Esther, a Jew, who used her position with her Persian husband, King Xerxes, to save her people from destruction, you must use your power and influence over the captains and kings of industry to provide jobs, contracts, and opportunities for our people. Ask God for direction. Read the Book of Esther in the Bible.

You are on the plantation just like Black men are. The only difference is, you're working in the big house while your men are out in the fields. You do not own the corporations, you merely work for them. Whether you like it or not, we are in this same boat together. In the spirit of healing and reconciliation, I offer you the following tips on assuming your rightful place in the family.

Don't allow yourself to be used. Did you know that corporate America fills their affirmative action requirements when they hire you? In the meantime, Black men have some of the highest unemployment rates in the country.

Don't forget where you are, Black woman. You're in America. If you must take that job, use it to learn all that you can. Then prepare a game plan to start your own.

Don't forget who you are. Even with your success, you must not lose your identity. As long as you live in America, you will always be Black and female. Return to your rightful place in the family and history will portray you as the strength, core, and glue of the African American family.

Return to chastity. Promiscuity has led too many Black women down the path of immorality, poverty, single parenthood, and disease. Today, you must return to the morals taught by your foremothers and the church. And then you must pass the lessons down to your children. Teach your daughter how to respect herself and her body by refusing to have sex before marriage. Teach your son how to respect himself, his body, and the females in his life. Tell him that even if a female disrespects herself that he must behave with integrity. He does not have to go there with her.

Raise your sons. Almost half of our households are maintained by women. The problem with young African American males is that they have no African American males to learn from. When husbands and wives come together to raise their sons (and daughters), healthy, happy children will be produced. With half of our families being raised by single African American women, however, we must seek new ways to raise our boys to manhood. For example, single mothers should seek out mature, healthy African American men to help raise their sons (and daughters).

Jawanza Kunjufu says, "Mothers love their sons and raise their daughters." Single Black mothers must love and raise their sons. Without a man in the home, the son often substitutes for the husband. This is inappropriate. Mothers and sons must keep the parent-child roles in focus at all times. Your son is a man in training, but he is not a man and he is surely not your husband.

Teach your son how to be responsible. Don't give him everything. Make him work. Don't make your daughter do all the work around the house. Give your son chores to do too. And when he gets a summer or after-school job, teach him how to allocate his paychecks for saving, tithing, and contributing to the home. Do not clothe him with chains and high-priced designer "gear." Even though the pressure will be on from an early age to dress according to the trends, help him develop self-esteem so that as he gets older, he won't feel the need to fit in with the crowd.

We all want our children's lives to be better than ours, but a soft life will not prepare them for the rigors of the world once they have left your protective wings. Through tough love, young males will be taught to earn their keep. This is the definition of manhood.

 Single mothers, do not allow your sons or daughters to see you getting in or out of bed with every Tom, Dick, and Harry. Stop telling your children, "I'd rather see you drink or smoke at home rather than in the streets." Stop giving them birth control to prevent pregnancy. Instead, tell them not to have sex!

Manage your money wisely. Don't get into the trap of living paycheck to paycheck. Black women often spend beyond their means on grooming and entertainment. Invest your money in ways that will ensure growth. Purchase items that will appreciate in value. Get your spending under control! Become a producer, and leave the consuming behind.

Use your income to build your family, church, and community. As one of the fastest growing groups starting their own businesses, you have the golden opportunity to do well. According to a 1996 report prepared by the National Foundation for Women Business Owners (NFWBO), "13 percent of the nearly 8 million women-owned businesses in the U. S. are owned by minority women. As of 1996, 37 percent

(405,200 women-owned firms) were held by Blacks. They employed 261,400 people and generated $24.7 billion in sales."[1] Furthermore, African American women are starting and running companies in nontraditional arenas, "including construction, wholesale trade, transportation, communications, and public utilities."[2]

Help resurrect the African American male. You are enjoying the same income and status in corporate America that was once reserved for African American men, albeit briefly. You seem to be surviving beyond the death of affirmative action. When we held this position, we did not forget you. We provided for you and loved you. Don't forget us. If you know of vacant positions in your company, recommend a brother for the job. We need your love and support now more than ever. Support us and help us reclaim our self-respect and self-esteem.

What Men Must Do

African American men, our families are totally dysfunctional. We no longer have a culture of marriage and family. Here's the picture:

- The African American divorce rate is higher than the marriage rate.
- More families are headed by females than males.
- Teenager pregnancy continues to be a problem. Studies are showing that girls who have fathers in the home are less inclined to have premarital sex and get pregnant as a teen.
- The average age of grandparents is lower than ever before.
- Children are telling parents what to do.
- Children are raising themselves.

Just as African American women must come back home, you must do the same. You must become a daily presence in the home. No longer can you be a rolling stone, laying down your hat and calling it home. God has given you a special assignment. You are to have dominion over the earth, sea, moon, and stars. While mother is at home taking care of the family, you must be about the business of making a living for the family. At the end of your work day, you are to come home. That's right, home. Men, I know this sounds like a strange idea, but you must actually live in the same house with your wife and family. Otherwise, you are not a family.

If you were ever needed in the home, you're needed now. Mother should be able to depend on you to share in disciplining responsibilities. When she says, "Our child has not done what he or she was supposed to do," she's telling you, "I need your help. I can't do it alone." Make your presence known with your children. There was a time when fathers put the fear of God in their children. Just one look was enough to correct bad behavior. But if you're nowhere to be found, your children will not mind you or respect you.

Not only are you needed for discipline, you are needed for your love. No one on earth can love a child or a woman like a Black man. It does not take away from your masculinity to love. Quite the opposite. You must demonstrate what tough love is all about. You must be tender and firm, fair and judicial, kind and tough, all rolled into one. Hard to do but absolutely necessary to build and strengthen our families.

Many men believe that being head of the household is an easy ticket to being a tyrant. Just because you are head of the household does not mean that you can abuse your authority. Domestic violence against women and children are secret, yet widespread problems in our community. Why would you abuse, batter, and beat up your woman and offspring? Are

you jealous of her success in our racist society? Are y
of corporate failure?

Whatever your hang-up, you must stop beating and abusing African American females. You must show her peace, joy, caring, and a true and sincere love. You must show a special love for her as the mother of your child or children, present or future. Make a committed effort to start today to show this love. Give surprise gifts of love—dinner at a nice restaurant, a card, flowers, a new dress. Give her time alone. Sometimes solitude is more precious than gold. Give often and give from the heart, with love and sincerity. Tell her "I love you." Listen to her when she's trying to talk to you. When her hair is pretty and freshly combed, tell her how pretty it is and how good she looks. Compliment her on her new dress or perfume.

Most important, communicate with her on all issues that concern the family. Share yourself with her. Tell her your innermost secrets. Learn how to argue well. You don't have to yell to get your point across. Don't take out your frustrations on her or the children. Being arrogant won't get you anything but her resentment. Kindness and understanding, on the other hand, works. I once heard a minister say that if more men said "my bad" to their wives like they do on the basketball court, more marriages would be saved. If you're wrong, apologize. If she's wrong, don't go off. Let her know how you feel. Your spouse should be your best friend.

Brothers, we have the most gorgeous, most intelligent women on the face of the earth. They deserve our love and commitment. They also deserve our patience.

Many Black women are shell shocked. They have experienced bad marriages and relationships. They are afraid to talk to and date Black men, even though it may have been years since their last relationship. Some are in abusive relationships and are afraid to tell someone for fear of reprisals.

African American men, I admonish you, if you do not love your women, let them go. Do not scar them for life by keeping them dangling, promising them love and affection when you really have none to give them. Let them go so that someone else can love them for whom they are.

It is God's will that we marry, raise our families, and stay committed and monogamous to our wives until we die, so choose your wife well. We were appointed to be head of our families. It is time we assumed our rightful place in the home. You've done it your way for so long. Why not try God's way?

Reason 11—Lack of Spiritual Vision

The most influential institution in the Black community is the Black church. It is the largest in number, finances, and membership. The future of our race depends on the Black church and its leadership. For that reason, I am very concerned about the Black church.

Jawanza Kunjufu writes that we have three types of churches—liberation, entertainment, and containment. Liberation churches are defined as those with a liberation theology of feeding the hungry, clothing the naked and preaching the gospel to the poor. Liberation churches attract a greater percentage of men and youth. They are open seven days a week and women are also in leadership positions.

I commend these churches and our community would not be in shambles if all of our 85,000 churches were liberation churches. Our problem is that the majority of our churches are not liberation churches. Unfortunately, they are entertainment and containment churches.

Entertainment churches sing, dance, shout, and hoop, but do little to empower the community. Containment churches are only opened on Sundays and Wednesdays. These churches are filled with elders and women. They have few programs for men and youth.

The African American church must return to its rightful position in our culture as our cornerstone and pillar of strength. Jawanza Kunjufu says that

> The last institution, reported by the University of Michigan study, influencing children was the church.

It has often been said that Black people survived slavery because of the family and the church. The comparative study between 1950 and 1992 reflects a declining influence of the church. The church in 1950 ranked third behind home and school, but now ranks last. What has happened to the church?[1]

In 1794, Richard Allen founded Bethel African Methodist Episcopal (A.M.E.) Church in Philadelphia, the first African American church in the country.[2] The establishment of Bethel A.M.E. was our first real act of self-determination.

The African American Church is still the one institution in our community that is independent, powerful, and influential. So why is it so out of touch with the needs of our people? Earlier, I spoke of the rampant ego problems of church leadership that has been undermining the growth and prosperity of our community. Ego has driven many church leaders down the road to self gratification and greed. Just remember, leaders, pride comes before the fall. Keep it up and you are destined to take a dive.

Remember why you were first called into the ministry? Have you totally forgotten what God has called you to do? You are to teach us how to love one another with an *agape*, unconditional love. In his book *Stride Toward Freedom*, Dr. King stated his belief that the Black church must also involve itself in social action. Jesus did not content himself to stand at the podium every Sunday to preach. Every day he was among the masses, talking to them, healing their wounds, feeding the hungry. Courageously, he fought the money changers in the temple. "Every minister of the gospel has a mandate to stand up courageously for righteousness, to proclaim the eternal verities of the gospel, and to lead men from the darkness of falsehood and fear to the light of truth and love."[3]

Not only does God want us to feed his sheep with the word of God, but he wants us to go and spread the word through a universal Christian church. Denominationalism has divided Black people since Allen's founding of Bethel A.M.E. The truth is, your church is not superior to mine, and mine is no better than yours. No church is an island unto itself. We, all of our churches, form the body of Christ, and God is the head of us all. Charles Wesley reports that after the Civil War, Baptists were the strongest denomination among Blacks.[4] Yet, whether you are A.M.E., Baptist, Lutheran, Church of God in Christ, Presbyterian, or Full Gospel, we are all brothers and sisters in Christ. Let not our chosen denominations longer divide us as a people. After all, no one church has all the answers.

Church leaders, get back into right relationship with the tithes and offerings given by your congregation. You do not own the money, it is God's money. You are a steward over the money. God has appointed you to use the money to meet the needs of the people, not buy yourself one more fancy car or luxury vacation. Bring your accounting system up to the 21st century. Computerize your system and institute a system of checks and balances to prevent fraud.

Just as men and women cannot do it alone, individual churches cannot be effective as islands unto themselves. Church leaders must come together, sort through and resolve their differences, and move forward. Churches that insist on doing it alone block the blessings of the church and congregations.

Another block is corruption in the church. So many of our church leaders are corrupt that salvation and deliverance blessings are being blocked from the parishioners. Will God answer the pastor's prayer if he is caught up in wrongdoing? And what of your participation? Is there a conspiracy of silence in your church? Do people talk behind the backs of the leaders but do nothing about the corruption? You may very well be blocking your own blessing. Regardless of your position in the church, you must stand for righteousness. In other words, do the right thing.

There is no reason why our 85,000 churches cannot unite to resolve the problems in our community. Each one meets regularly, on Sundays. Each one solicits tithes and offerings. Each one is based in a community. Each and every Black church should share in the legacy of Allen and all the founding fathers: worshipping God and meeting the needs of people.

The Black church is rich and powerful, all it needs is a vision and direction. What if 10,000 or more of our churches donated $20.00 each Sunday, or $200,000 each week, for a poverty relief fund to be invested by an investment house? As an independent accounting entity, the investment house would keep our leaders honest. When the Lord sees that we are serious about solving our problems then He will unblock our blessings.

Individually, many Black churches are already wealthy. Together, they would be an unbeatable force for good. And if the Body of Christ formed alliances with other groups in the Black community—sororities and fraternities, for example—we would have at our disposal a vast repository of spiritual power and financial wealth to rival the Federal Reserve.

When the African American church and its leaders begin to change from their evil ways, repent of their sins, seek God's face, and pray, then they will hear from heaven and heal this land. Only then will the blessings that are stored for us begin to flow.

In earlier times, the Black Preacher fulfilled the role of Headman with a grave sense of responsibility and accountability both to his African American congregation and to God. During those earlier times, the commitment of the Black Preacher allowed the Black Church to build universities, provide financial support to the poor, instill a powerful work ethic, establish and sustain a strong moral code, and support and protect the sanctity of home and family.

Unfortunately, as time passed, the Black Preacher became increasingly more self-centered and self-focused. As the mechanism of social integration, direction, and control he stopped expressing the consensus of the congregation.

He accomplished this by taking on the role of Shaman in addition to his role as Headman. Though the Bible clearly states that the Holy Spirit is the agent by which believers have direct access to God, the Black Preacher used misdirection and perversion of the Holy Scriptures to make the congregation believe that without him, they had no direct access to God. Without him they could not possibly know God's will. In short, the Black Preacher proclaimed himself "priest," a role that in Protestantism is distinctly one that belongs to Jesus Christ.

Once the self-serving Black Preacher became both Headman and Shaman, he possessed the most complete power a leader can possess over the congregation. He has demonstrated beyond dispute that such power corrupts. At this time in history, the Black Preacher is not so much an under shepherd of Jesus Christ but one of the false prophets of Matthew 7:15 who comes in sheep's clothing but who are inwardly ravening wolves.

In these times of the self-serving, self-focused Headman-Shaman Black Preacher, the consensus of the congregation has been re-molded. Instead of following God's agenda, the congregation has been tricked into following the Black Preacher's agenda. Our community cannot grow with pastors like Henry Lyons, former leader of the National Baptist Convention. Sadly, it took the government to remove him because the Baptists and his congregation did not.

God's agenda for his church is clearly stated in the Scriptures and includes, conforming believers to the image of Christ, supporting the needs of widows and orphans, feeding the hungry, clothing the naked, housing the homeless, and visiting the incarcerated and the sick.

The Black church's agenda as defined and enforced by the Black Preacher includes the weekly assembly of large numbers of people. Though the Bible clearly teaches that God is present where two or three are gathered, the Black Preacher strongly encourages the weekly assembly of large numbers of people. The reason for this is three-fold.

First of all the more people who are present, the larger the potential economic benefit to the Black Preacher. The more bodies that assemble for the Sunday Morning Extravaganza, the more money that is likely to be transferred from the control of individual members of the congregation to the control of the Black Preacher.

Secondly, Black Preachers engage in a weekly pissing contest with each other based on their ability to attract the largest number of bodies on a Sunday morning. A Black Preacher that can consistently attract 2,000 bodies undoubtedly has more personal charisma and magnetism than one who can attract only a few dozen.

A third item on the Black Preacher's agenda is entertaining the congregation. Church layouts are ideally suited for entertainment. In fact, most sanctuaries look like theaters. They have seats for the audience facing a stage-like pulpit both ideal for dramatic and comedic entertainment. At this point in African American history, entertainment is an integral part of the Sunday Morning Extravaganza. So conditioned is the congregation by the Black Preacher that if he fails to have a really slamin', jamin', rockin' rollin' choir to back him up on Sunday morning, the congregation usually grows restless and eventually moves on to a place where the choir does rock and roll.

Furthermore, the standard of success for the Black Preacher himself is based in large degree on his performance, i.e., the emotional impact of his sermon, his delivery, his attractiveness, his personal magnetism. When the Black Preacher has all these things working for him, he usually enjoys the status of celebrity with his congregation and beyond.

The glorification of a man is the fourth agenda item. For many African Americans of limited economic means and education, the Black Church is the only place where they can attain any power whatsoever. Knowing this, the Black Preacher uses these appointments as tools of manipulation. He has the power to put people into positions of leadership and/or authority within the Black Church. These appointments are generally made on the basis of the Black Preacher's personal criteria. Often these appointments are made to reward loyalty or as a strategy for strengthening the Black Preacher's position or for manipulating circumstances to his advantage. These appointments can even be used as ruses to make it easier to conduct sexual liaisons.

Yet another agenda item is the purchase of real estate to be controlled by the Black Preacher. This is necessary so that bigger and grander building can be built to house the large number of bodies drawn to the Sunday Morning Extravaganza and ultimately the collection plate.

If the agenda of the Black Church were consistent with God's plan rather than consistent with the self-serving, self-centered Headman-Shaman Black Preacher's perversion of that plan, there would be no need for any African Americans to be on welfare. The congregation would be committed to the Lord's command to feed the hungry, house the homeless, clothe the naked, to care for the widows and orphans—particularly if the concept of widows and orphans were expanded to include divorced and unwed mothers and their children.

If the agenda of the Black Church were consistent with God's plan the gravest attention would be given to teaching by example a high moral code that embraced righteousness and rejected unrighteousness. This means that doing the right thing would be expected of the congregation and the Headman without exception—every time, all the time, no matter what. While God's children, like God himself, are to be forgiving, they are not to tolerate (as a group) immorality and unrighteousness—particularly among their leaders. Thus when righteousness is rejected and moral and ethical codes are violated, such behavior should be rejected loudly and unashamedly regardless of who is involved. If the Black Church would follow God's agenda in this regard, African America would be morally strong, spiritually grounded, and a powerful force to be reckoned with.

If the agenda of the Black Church were consistent with God's plan, the millions of dollars that are transferred from the control of the individual members of the congregation to the control of the Black Preacher would be pooled and used to promote the Kingdom of God rather than the interests of the Black Preacher.

Sadly, African Americans as a group are on a one-way road to New Slavery. This road is constructed of moral decay, ethical bankruptcy, and economic impotence. The Black Church is the vehicle and the self-serving, self-centered, Head-man-Shaman-Black Preacher is at the wheel with his foot jamming the accelerator into the floorboard. It's time to hi-jack the bus!

I appeal to you pastors. Who called you? Have you completed seminary from an accredited college? Are you developing a liberation church? Our communities need strong moral leaders with vision to follow Jesus.

Reason 12—Confusion About the Purpose of African American Sororities and Fraternities

Congratulations are in order for African American sororities and fraternities on coming together to develop and implement many worthy projects. (Maybe you could share some of your insights with the African American church.)

According to *The National Directory of African American Organizations 1998-2000*, there are a total of 13 sororities and fraternities, with 947,000 members and 5,711 chapters combined.[1] The system is impressive in its ability to generate revenue and solicit new members.

In 1930, the National Pan Hellenic Council was established at Howard University as a national coordinating body for the African American fraternities and sororities which were growing on college campuses across the country. Racism had barred Black students from joining White groups. As a result, the Black Greek system grew steadily. These organizations provided Black students a much needed social outlet that provided support and entertainment.

Fraternities and sororities, what is your role in the African American scheme of things? Are you serious about building the community? Or are you about partying and having a good time?

National and regional conventions sponsored by these groups generate millions of dollars in hotel, travel, and tourism dollars. Why not come together to create your own hotel? According to *Black Enterprise*, the Cendant Corporation, parent company of Days Inn, Ramada Inn, Travelodge, Howard Johnson, and others, are aggressively recruiting African Americans to start hotel chains.[2] With all the accountants, marketing professionals, managers, and entrepreneurs within your ranks, surely you could come together to develop a plan to purchase a hotel?

If 10,000 Deltas or Alpha Kappa Alphas met for three days, at $60.00 per person per day, they'd generate $1.8 million for the hotel. Forego your convention for one year and use that money to raise seed capital. In one year you'd have enough to make a respectable bid on a classy hotel. If you gave the money over to a money market fund manager, in two-three years, with a healthy rate of return, you could have as much as $5 to $10 million, even more. That's power.

Most African American organizations suffer from a lack of capital—no money to accomplish their goals. With a vision, unity, and good leadership, African American fraternities and sororities could have money to accomplish many worthwhile projects.

Here are some more ideas for building wealth:

♦ Every member donates one share of stock or a US Savings Bond annually to the organization, creating a fund of perpetuity assuring the life and growth of the organization.

♦ At the end of every seventh year, return one share or one bond to participating members. This would give new meaning to the terms "reciprocity" or "profit sharing."

The time is past for talking. You have it within your power to take action today. The African American community needs you to pull together. You've done great things, and it's time to do even more.

Reason 13—Lack of Investigative African American Media

Is the African American media censored? Seldom do we get the truth about what's going on in the world from our own media. We have to resort to other media, which reports questionable information at best. Our media is full of public relations pieces on celebrities, politicians, ministers, and entrepreneurs. In its attempt to counteract all the negative themes promoted by the general media, African American media has gone the other extreme by providing us nothing of substance.

What is the agenda of our media? African American magazines and books are out of touch with their reporting, analyses of the issues, and strategies for change. The goal is not to present African Americans in a negative light, but to provide the truth from an African-centered perspective. Reporting from this perspective would have as its goal understanding the truth and providing solutions to the problems. Today, our media outlets are nothing more than poor imitations of programs developed and hyped by the dominant culture. Our media has a responsibility to creatively portray our stories and our issues in positive, community-building ways.

Music

We don't need any more hip hop radio programs or music videos on TV—unless they are solution oriented. Music, which is a powerful, influential medium, has sunk so low as to promote misguided, misdirected, degrading, demoralizing songs glorifying gangs, drugs, materialism, and irresponsible sex. It's no mystery to me why our youth are acting out in so many negative ways. They are being persuaded, in part, by the music. African American producers, recording artists, radio programmers, dee jays, TV hosts, and retail outlets, you must elevate the quality of the music you produce, create, promote, and distribute. You've fallen down on the job, but there's no time like the present to change your ways.

You cannot be so driven by the acquisition of money and material goods that you forsake the health and welfare of our people. In your music, you present lyrics that inspire low morals, low self-esteem, death, and destruction. When you do the right thing, good things happen. Trust in God to fulfill your financial needs. Create music that uplifts us. Many rap artists say that they are merely reporting the conditions of the streets, but you don't have to rap that tune. You can point us all in a higher direction. To do that, you must be in tune with the Holy Spirit within. Pray for divine guidance and you will know which direction to take your music.

Television

According to Joseph L. White and Thomas A. Parham in *The Psychology of Blacks*,

> Exposure to massive amounts of television on a daily basis has been identified as one of the prime socializers of African American youngsters. In subtle and some not so subtle ways, our children's value systems are being influenced and shaped by what they visually and auditorily absorb from that medium. This realization is compounded by the notion that Black children devote a disproportionately high

amount of time to television viewing (as high as six hours per day) and, like other children, are likely to believe that television accurately reflects life as it really is or should be.[1]

Jawanza Kunjufu says that the second greatest competitor for the minds of our children is television.[2] Many experts believe television is the number one influencer of young minds. With its fast-moving pictures and music, television is highly appealing to children. If their viewing times are not monitored, children will sit in front of the TV during every waking moment. Some studies indicate that Black children watch the most TV out of all the racial groups. No wonder our children have been acting out.

It is projected that in the 1999-2000 television line-up, for the first time in decades there will be no lead roles for African American actors. Instead of moving forward we are moving back. Our TV watching children are learning their life lessons from people who don't even look like them. This is a problem. It is critical that our children have positive role models to emulate and African-centered themes to learn from. Fighting on the Hollywood front is the NAACP in Beverly Hills. Call the NAACP and find out how you can support their effort for fair and equal representation on television.

Radio

Radio is also important. The research about the effects of radio on youth is not as extensive as television, but given the lyrics in the music our children listen to, it's equally alarming. African American urban music is sexually suggestive, disrespectful of women, full of foul language, and glorifies violence and the drug culture.

The African American media, we're looking to you to provide solid information, *truthful* information. We need this information to educate our young people, heal ourselves, start new businesses, and uplift ourselves morally and spiritually. Let people like Tony Brown and Tavis Smiley take the lead. Their programs are unashamedly pro-Black. In every medium there are African Americans who, despite the current trends, support our cause. They deserve our support and our gratitude.

Reason 14—Lack of
Business Resources

There is a strong entrepreneurial spirit in the African American community, but often we do not fully appreciate the hard work and long hours (60 to 100 hours per week) that is required to succeed. It may take awhile before you're able to enjoy the fruit of your labor. Your own people won't support you. Racism at banking institutions prohibits fair lending. We often lack knowledge of basic business practices in such areas as accounting, law, taxation, marketing, and other areas. So if you're starting your own company for the status and prestige that comes with being "President and CEO," then think again.

According to Charles Wesley, at the turn of the century, "A sizable number of imaginative Negroes entered various small business ventures and took the lead in gaining cooperation to form larger firms. The small-scale establishments included grocery stores, barber shops, restaurants and funeral homes. Large businesses were few, since the Negro businessman had little capital and creditors persisted in regarding him as a poor risk."[1]

Each year, *Black Enterprise* publishes its list of the top African American companies, but we have a long way to go. We still have little working capital and creditors consider us a poor risk. You need capital and credit to start a business and to make it grow. No matter how good your idea is, you'll never make it out of the starting gate without money.

According to reporter Gene Koretz,

A National Bureau of Economic Research study revealed that Blacks were almost twice as likely to have a loan application denied than Whites. They also found that black companies pay higher interest rates.[2]

We cannot give up our dreams because of racism. John H. Johnson started his empire with a $500 loan from his mother. We can succeed, despite the hurdles. Here are my recommendations for dealing with the capital issue.

Develop a plan. If you don't have a carefully thought out, well-written plan of action, you won't know where you're going. If you don't have a plan, no lender will even meet with you. A plan helps you think strategically about what you want to accomplish in your company. First, write a brief mission statement which describes the purpose of your company. Then, set goals (revenue, marketing, etc.) and the action steps to achieve those goals (make sure to include timelines). Then *take action.*

Start small. We want to make millions right away, but that's only possible in your dreams. The reality is, unless you inherit your money, you will have to start small. Many of our businesses were started in a basement, a garage, the street corner. Millionaire Madame C. J. Walker researched her popular hair care products right in her own kitchen. Keep your overhead to a minimum.

Manage your personal finances. Robert Townsend did the impossible: he produced his first movie, *Hollywood Shuffle,* with credit cards. He had to have good credit to do it. If you've got bad personal credit, you're going to have a tough time getting business credit. Remember, creditors are looking for the smallest of reasons to discriminate against you. One late payment and they will cut you loose in a minute.

Beg and borrow from friends and family. Form strategic alliances. In the spirit of *ujamaa,* cooperative economics, present your idea to all who know you and offer them an opportunity to profit with you. Develop relationships with others who are in complimentary fields and pool your resources. For example, if you both need a copier, split the cost on rental.

Seek out an influential mentor. Get advice from African Americans who know your business and who have made mistakes and learned from them. They may even know about secret sources of money that you can tap into.

Create a national African American venture capital fund. Obtaining capital is the number one problem that African American entrepreneurs face. So why not take the lead and approach African American churches, established entrepreneurs, and stock brokers and money market managers with a proposal to create a venture capital fund to provide seed money for struggling entrepreneurs. All it takes is one person to get the ball rolling.

Self-employment is demanding, but it is also rewarding. With persistence and a little ingenuity, you can achieve your dreams. More than money, you need self-confidence and faith in God, because it is a risk. But the only way to know whether your idea will prosper is to do it.

After so many years of self-employment my youngest son told me, "Dad, the law of averages ought to be in your favor by now." Sure, there will be failures, but learn from them, don't allow them to get you down. Get up and try again.

Many of us are called to entrepreneurship, but few are chosen. We all have dreams, but few take the risks necessary to achieve their dreams. Many people dream their life away, and then, in their later years, they are bitter with regret. Don't let this happen to you. Take a chance on your dream, but in the beginning stages, heed this word of advice: Don't quit your day job!

Reason 15—Insurance

There are many necessary evils in life, and life insurance is one of them. There is something about paying for something that *might* happen that rubs us the wrong way. But insurance is necessary to provide for your loved ones in case of your death.

It has been said that African Americans do not believe in purchasing life insurance. Is it because we're a "live in the moment" kind of people? If you died tomorrow, who would pay for your burial? Your bills? It is irresponsible to bequeath a financial burden, instead of blessing, to your family. Check your policy (if you have one). Is the payoff large enough to cover burial costs, debt, your children's education, etc.? Probably not. Do not take the value of insurance lightly. Today it's a necessary evil, but tomorrow it will be a godsend for your loved ones.

If your income will be missed after your untimely death, you need some insurance. That's a fact that's all the more important if your children are minors. 'Don't go by the rules of thumb, 'such as buy six times your income in life insurance. Secure the opinion of a certified financial planner. Determine what your family's income needs will be, what sources of income will be available and how much life insurance will be necessary to provide the income that will be lacking.

There are two basic types of insurance: whole life and term. Whole life insurance costs more. There is a savings feature contained within the policy. The interest rate is very low and if you borrow money from your policy, they force you to repay or deduct it from the policy.

Term insurance has no hidden savings or loan features attached. Like they say, buy term insurance and invest the difference. Many agents sell African Americans whole life because it's more expensive, they earn a larger commission, and the assumption that African Americans will not invest the difference if they bought the less expensive term insurance.

A New Vision for Life Insurance

Rather than insuring people against the eventuality of their death, why not insure that we live a long healthy, happy life? Wouldn't it be great if there was a policy that was designed to *protect* the lives of African American young people who are so hell bent on destroying themselves and each other? We could call it *living insurance*. In order to achieve the payoff of a long and happy life, the following stipulations would have to be met by the insured:

- ♦ Must graduate from high school.
- ♦ Must go to college.
- ♦ Must refrain from using drugs, alcohol, and tobacco products.
- ♦ Must not get into a gang.
- ♦ Must strive to be a model citizen.
- ♦ Cannot have any babies out of wedlock.
- ♦ Must not disrespect parents.

In addition to the above-mentioned payoffs, the insured might receive a downpayment on a new home, a scholarship to pursue graduate studies, or seed money to start a company. Payoff would be on the insured's 35th birthday. Such a policy would give our young people something to look forward to. Instead of racing toward an early demise, they would work toward a beautiful future.

Reason 16—Interracial Marriage

"A man should leave his father and mother, and be forever united to his wife. Two shall become one—no longer two, but one! And no man may divorce what God has joined together."—Matthew 19:5, 9

"You honor Christ by submitting to each other. Wives must submit to your husbands' leadership in the same way you submit to the Lord....And you husbands, show the same kind of love to your wives as Christ showed to the Church when he died for her."
—Ephesians 5:21, 22, 25–28; Proverbs 31

Within the past 30 years, since the passing of the Civil Rights Laws, there has been an increase of interracial relationships. Despite the growth, there are still people who are offended by seeing Black men and women with people of other races. So beware, if you decide to marry a person of another race, there will be problems. You must have a strong love, unity, and understanding to carry you through. In his *Ebony* advice column, Dr. King gave this counsel on interracial marriages:

Properly speaking, races do not marry, individuals marry. There is nothing morally wrong with an interracial marriage. There are many other things, however, that must be taken under consideration in any interracial marriage. The traditions of our society have been so set and crystallized that many social obstacles stand in the way of persons involved in an interracial marriage. If persons entering such a marriage are thoroughly aware of these obstacles and feel that they have the power and stability to stand up amid them, then there is no reason why these persons should not be married. Studies reveal that interracial couples who have come together with a thorough understanding of conditions that exist, have married and lived together very happily.[1]

Frequent association can create friendship. When you sit down and communicate with another person, you get to know him or her inside or out. You find out if you like, or even love, the person. True love is like good music which transcends all barriers—color lines, racial and ethnic backgrounds, and languages. True love is 99% color blind.

If marriage is the next logical step in a growing, loving relationship, the two partners must discuss some serious issues. For example, does your partner know about the One Drop Law—i.e., one drop of Black blood makes you Black, and that means your children. Biracial children suffer in our racist society, even in this day and age of skin tanning and enlarged lips. How will you raise your child to develop self-esteem in such a hostile society?

Love is a beginning, but it is not enough. I highly recommended that the two of you invite God Almighty into your lives to direct, guide, and protect your marriage. Trust God and He will surely bless your marriage and your children.

Reason 17—Poor Health

The prognosis for African American health is bleak. According to the Council of Economic Advisers for the President's Initiative on Race, "The state of African American health is scoring below every other race in the United States. One of the reasons for this difference is that on the average, white Americans have better access to the social and economic resources necessary for healthy environments and lifestyles and better access to preventive medical services."[1]

African Americans are much too sedentary. As a result, we have among the highest obesity rates in the country. Obesity leads to many *preventable* problems in the body, including heart disease, diabetes, arthritis, and more. African American men have the highest rates of hypertension.

Cardiovascular disease, which includes heart disease and stroke, is the cause of 40 percent of all deaths in the United States. One million Americans die every year. It is the number one killer of African Americans. According to the National Institute of Neurological Disorders and Stroke, hypertension and diabetes are almost twice as great among African Americans as whites. At one time, hypertension was considered an old person's disease, but that has changed dramatically mainly because of poor eating habits.[2]

It's time to get up and get moving. You might not want to hear this, but I'm going to tell you anyway. We must make exercise a part of our culture, or we're going to die. Not only is exercise necessary to deal with obesity and related ailments, it relieves stress. Being Black in a racist society, we need all the stress relief we can get.

Getting our stress under control is a challenge. Our community suffers from high unemployment, discrimination, poor housing, poor health care, inferior education, and low quality foods. Many of us eat to calm our nerves. We eat greasy foods at the fast food restaurants that abound in our neighborhoods. The foods we love are full of sugar, salt, and chemicals such as MSG (monosodium glutamate). Our diet is high in red meat, a known killer and cancer causer. This constant indulging in low-octane food, combined with the lack of exercise produces heaviness, lack of energy, lack of self-esteem, and illness.

To remedy this situation, I challenge our dieticians, scientists, naturopaths, and doctors to study 10,000 high risk African American males for five years. Divide this group into two groups of 5,000. Give each male in Group A a job paying $40,000 per year. Give each male in Group B a job paying minimum wage. Establish your research criteria and set your controls. Periodically monitor the physical vital signs and psychological health of each male. At the end of the five-year period, which group will have the best average blood pressure rate—the group of men who were paid a respectable wage with health insurance and other benefits or the men who were barely able to pay the rent and care for their families on their minimum wage salaries?

Dennis Kimbro says that "You cannot separate the body and the mind, for they are one. Anything that affects the health and vigor of the mind will affect the body. In turn, anything that affects the health of the body will affect the mind."[3]

Many writers and health professionals are sounding the alarm, but are we listening? Norma Chappell doesn't think so. "Today, African Americans are dying younger from diseases than ever before. These diseases, if caught in their early stages, have a higher survival rate, but because African Americans are not practicing preventive health, they are dying prematurely."[4] Chappell lists the top ten killer diseases of African Americans:

1. Heart Disease
2. Cancer
3. Cerebrovascular (Stroke)
4. HIV/AIDS (Human Immunodeficiency Virus)
5. Diabetes
6. Influenza and Pneumonia
7. Birth Defects
8. Chronic Obstructive Lung Disease
9. Nephritis (Kidney Disease)
10. Septicemia (Blood Disease)[5]

If you are looking for a quick fix, you're not going to find it here. Thousands of diet and so-called health books have been written, promising glowing results with minimal effort. The only way to wean yourself from your hypertension medicine, the only detour from the sure road to the graveyard, is to exercise, relieve stress (try prayer), and eat nutritional, natural, meat-free foods. When was the last time you had a good sweat from exercise? Exercise needn't cost you one cent. Just put on your gym shoes and go for a walk, jog, or run, depending on your fitness level. If you haven't been working out, check in with your doctor first. Even the most out-of-shape individuals usually get the consent of their doctor to begin a walking program.

You also need to get eight hours of sleep each night. No more staying up late to party. Go to bed, and get some sleep! The older you get, the less you're able to stay up all hours of the night, hanging out with your friends and drinking. We must redefine "good time." Let a good time for you be eight hours of restful, peaceful sleep.

Cut the booze. African Americans cannot afford to waste their precious time in bars, dulling their brains with alcohol. Alcohol can damage the liver. According to Alfred Powell, it is a "chemical castrator."[6] Night clubbing also puts a drain on the pocketbook. What kind of a message is that to send to our young people? If we expect them to behave respectably, we must check our own behavior. We must be good role models for our children and mankind in general. We must raise our morals and values, and we must begin to practice what we preach.

Don't do drugs. Illegal drugs are the worst scourge to plague the African American community. They have never helped anyone truly feel good or escape from their problems. Leave them alone. Follow my Four Commandments and you'll enjoy long life and good health:

SMOKE NOT.
DRINK NOT.
INJECT NOT.
SNORT NOT.

Reason 18—Loss of Identity

Who do you think you are? Are you Black? African American? Or just plain American? With integration came a loss of our sense of identity. There was a time in the not so distant past when we knew who we were—because we were subjected to enforced segregation. Just one tiny drop of Black blood was enough to make you live on the Black side of town or make you send your children to the Black school.

We built this country, we have a right to enjoy all the privileges our citizenship conveys. That does not mean we stop being Black. You'll never be able to change the color of your skin, nor should you want to. Your color is an important part of who you are as an individual. Yet, even at the dawn of a new millennium, many of us still hate ourselves and would change the color of our skin if we could. Some of us think that a lighter skin color would make them feel better. Don't you know that everybody wants what you have naturally? Your hair, lips, hips, style, and color—all the physical and intangible characteristics that identify you as Black. You should be proud! While others are risking skin cancer, God graced you with a beautiful darkness.

Remember that old study that found that little Black girls prefer White dolls to dark-skinned dolls? That's not such an old study! It's still the case today.

Don't let your pursuit of the American Dream make you forget your identity. By all means, improve your surroundings but never forget where you came from or how you got there. You may have to return one day.

Most important, don't forget *who* you are and to what race you belong. Why are we the only race to get amnesia when it comes to remembering our color and heritage? We were the first people on the face of the earth! We are unique and powerful. We were God's first creation on earth. All other races came from us.

Do you identify with the word "nigger?" Do you call your African American friends "nigger?" Webster's New Collegiate Dictionary defines the word "nigger" as any member of any dark-skinned race, so we must redefine the word for ourselves. You are not a "nigger" because of your skin color. You are not a "nigger" at all. Let us understand this word to mean "low life attitude." Now, does that sound like you? Vow to eliminate the word from your vocabulary. From this day, resolve to never call anyone that word again.

Carter G. Woodson said that miseducation about our true greatness is the source of our confusion about identity. Here are my recommendations to reconcile yourself to the fact that you are Black, of the Black race, will always and forever be Black.

1. Seek God Almighty first.
2. Educate yourself on the history and accomplishments of the African race.
3. Unify economically.
4. Develop a good work ethic.
5. Stick to a savings plan.
6. Strive for good health.
7. Choose African American role models.
8. Develop fashion and grooming styles that flatter your African features.

We can begin to feel good about our color and our membership in a great race by simply looking in the mirror and appreciating our African features. Choose today to identify with greatness.

Reason 19—Integration

In hindsight we now know that integration has been hazardous to our cultural health. When we integrated with White people, we assimilated into their culture and left our own behind. Thanks to integration, we are raising our children according to Western values instead of African-centered ones. With the birth of each new generation comes the further erosion of the values that made us strong and that kept us together as a people.

The disturbing behavior of our children is due in large part to our having integrated and assimilated into White society. They no longer respect their parents, and they don't understand that freedom is never free, that it comes with responsibilities. We have not told them our stories, so they have no appreciation for our heritage and culture.

Their fixation on achieving wealth and material goods is in direct contrast to the African way of communal living and spiritual enlightenment. Greed has created an emptiness in our children and no appreciation for life. That's why a mere brush on the shoulder or accidental step on the gym shoe can result in a bullet in the head.

We left the education of our children up to the public school system. As a result, our children do not enjoy learning. They drop out of school at high rates. They believe that school is no longer relevant to their lives. Remember how at the turn of the century our foreparents went after learning with a vengeance because it had been denied them in slavery? What would they think of us now? They must be turning in their graves.

Many African Americans born after Brown vs. Topeka (1954) and the March on Washington (1963) believe that their parents and the world owe them something—a high paying job, an expensive imported car, a big home in the suburbs, and vacations in Europe. Where did they get this idea from? Their parents! Who doesn't want their children to have life a bit easier? Our elders grew up in the Jim Crow era of lynchings and blatant discrimination. Survival was a day-to-day challenge. Of course they didn't want their children to suffer as they did.

The problem is, they went too far. They gave their children too much. Parents, you owe your children love and a stable home environment. That's it. You don't have to buy them a car upon graduation or a trip to some God-forsaken place. Let them earn their own way. When they do succeed in life, they'll better appreciate their success because they worked for it.

Children are also getting wrong ideas from television, so turn it off! Black children watch too much TV anyway.

Focus on teaching your children good morals. Teach them strong Christian values. Teach them to pray. Teach them to respect their bodies through good nutrition and exercise. If they are to go beyond you, let them do it the old-fashioned way: through hard work and determination.

Unfortunately, we cannot turn back the hands of time. Integration is a reality in our lives. However, you can take steps to minimize the negative affects of Western culture on yourself and your children.

1. Attend an African American church.
2. Participate in community events.
3. Honor family traditions, such as family reunions.
4. Study the works of Black scholars.
5. Seek out friendships with other African Americans on the job.

6. Join a Black book club.
7. Listen to good Black music with positive lyrics, such as Gospel.
8. Purchase goods and services from African American entrepreneurs.
9. Make a donation of time or money to a worthy Black organization such as the NAACP, PUSH, or UNCF.

The moral of this story is, you cannot integrate from a position of weakness. Integration does not have to be synonymous with assimilation. We must become strong and unified first. We must feel secure in and good about our African identities first. Then and only then should you form alliances with other groups, always keeping in mind the good of the race.

Reason 20—Ignorance About African American Contributions to Science and Technology

If we are to believe mainstream history books and media, African Americans never invented any tool, product, or service to enhance the quality of life. Like Malcolm X said, you've been bamboozled, hoodwinked! Around the turn of the century, during some of the most difficult times we've ever experienced, African Americans were busy inventing and unlocking the secrets of nature.

As a Philadelphia shoemaker's apprentice, J.E. Matzeliger invented a shoe lasting machine that revolutionized the industry. Prior to his invention, shoes had to be put together by hand and would take hours, even days, to complete a pair. Matzeliger's machine nailed the shoe in place and delivered a finished product in less than a minute. Because of racism, he was not able to garner support to form his own company. Sadly, he sold his invention to the United Shoe Company of Boston, which, thanks to Matzeliger's time saving device, became the largest shoe company of the time.[1]

An African American was instrumental in developing a device that you and I use every day. Lewis Latimer, an engineer and inventor from New York, worked with Alexander Graham Bell to create the telephone. In fact, Latimer made the drawings for Bell's first phone.[2] Now we know why African Americans love to talk all hours of the day and night on the telephone! Latimer also worked with Thomas Edison.

In 1872, Elijah McCoy patented an automatic lubricating cup for machines. He secured patents in later years for 57 inventions, most of which are in general use in lubricating machinery today.[3]

When it came to understanding electricity, Granville T. Woods was a genius. General Electric, Westinghouse Air Brake Company, and the Bell Telephone Company all bought patents from him.[4]

And we are still inventing, discovering, and creating today. African Americans are at the forefront of some of the most exciting research in telecommunications, software and hardware development, agriculture, not to mention medicine and other fields that enhance the quality of life for everyone. Sometimes African American geniuses are working in modest jobs, but are creating great and wonderful things for their companies and society—often to no benefit to themselves.

During the early 1970s in Indianapolis, Indiana, I became friends with DeLonzo Rhyne, Sr., an African American body shop manager of the Mustang Ranch. His job was to ensure the shop ran smoothly and to repair both American and foreign vehicles.

As he honed his mechanical skills, Rhyne developed a love of Ford Mustangs, especially models made during 1964 to 1969. He began to collect and restore them to factory specifications. Soon his yard was overflowing with Mustangs. To regular people it looked like a junk yard, but to Rhyne it was the Garden of Eden.

Now, my friend received numerous complaints from the city. They wanted him to get rid of the cars. Rhyne refused, and today, he has what is probably the largest collection of Mustangs in the country. But his collection is not the only thing that makes him special.

In the early stages of attempting to restore the Mustangs, Rhyne found it difficult to reach into certain areas of stripped down bodies that needed repair or replacement.

What he needed was a device that would lift the body off the floor as well as enable him to turn the body at different angles. He couldn't find a device that would meet his needs, so he created one. He designed and built a rotisserie-like device that lifted the car body approximately three feet off the floor. The design also allowed him to turn the body at any angle so that he could access hard-to-reach places. He named his creation the "UniStan." Truly an ingenious device.

On December 29, 1993, at the Indianapolis Convention Center, the Ford Motor Company paid homage to DeLonzo Rhyne at their big Reintroduction of the Mustang gala. The secret to his success? As Mr. Rhyne says, "necessity is the mother of invention." His future goals include restoring 20 Mustangs per year and selling them to lease companies.

My modest recounting of the great African American inventors only scratches the surface of what we have done and what we can do. It is critical that we groom children with a gift and interest in science and technology to invent products that will benefit society. We must encourage them by attending their school science fairs and not getting too angry when they cause a mess around the house with all their experimenting!

Just as we must support Black entrepreneurs, we must support our inventors and scientists. We must keep their accomplishments alive in our memories and in our school curricula. Whenever you stop at a red light, tell your children that a Black man designed the stoplight. Whenever you style your hair, remember Madam C. J. Walker.

A Plan to Groom Young Scientists and Inventors

1. Scientists and inventors, you must scout out new talent like college and professional basketball coaches. Look for the spark of genius in elementary schools, high

schools, colleges, universities, and technical and vocational schools.

2. African American churches, encourage scientific progress in your congregations. God gave us faith, and He also gave us minds. I'll bet there are children in your churches that would love to follow a doctor, an engineer, or a computer programmer around for a day. Start a mentoring program that pairs the professionals and youth in your churches.

3. Educators, create a program that will identify at least 12 gifted children in science and math. Take them on special field trips. Stage pep rallies for intellectual competitions, such as science and technology fairs. Pair your students with professionals in the community. Stimulate their minds and interests. You might discover the next Lewis Latimore or DeLonzo Rhyne!

4. African American medical colleges, scout out gifted students at local high schools and create a college preparatory program. Give scholarships to at least ten bright graduating seniors from economically disadvantaged families each year. Make your program as glamorous and fun as basketball.

Let not the efforts of the great ones such as Dr. George Washington Carver and Charles R. Drew go in vain. Dr. Carver had an outstanding record of training young scientists and we—not the government—must carry on his legacy.

Reason 21—Lack of Support from African American Athletes

The African American male athlete has truly arrived. In no other sector of American society have Black people been able to make their presence so strongly felt as in professional sports. Add to this domination the many multimillion dollar contracts athletes enjoy and you have a true phenomenon.

On many levels this success is well deserved. It takes hours of disciplined work every day to play as well as these men do and to achieve peak physical conditioning. Their ability to hold a crowd spellbound with their incredible feats of daring on the courts and fields of American stadiums generate billions of dollars for team owners and related industries. When Michael Jordan announced his reentry into basketball, his decision affected the stock market. That's just how powerful the Black athlete is today.

However, we cannot escape the fact that no matter how well paid these athletes are, their lives are not their own. If there are team owners, then there must be the "owned." Many have called Black athletes high priced slaves, and unfortunately it is true. The slavemaster doesn't have to whip his "boys" to keep them in line. The lure of fame, fortune, and plenty of women is enough to keep them dancing to the slavemaster's tune.

There was a time when African Americans would,

as a matter of course, return to the communities that reared them. Whether it was to establish a homebase in the old neighborhood, open a store, or mentor a child, we used to give back. Why? Because it was the right thing to do. Today, when a Black athlete makes it in the pro world, he seldom returns to the streets of his childhood. In fact, it seems the moment an African American athlete signs a major contract, he immediately divorces his wife and/or severs ties with the African American girlfriend, his family, and friends. We are the only people on the face of the earth who can forget what race they belong to.

Black athletes are mentally enslaved. They seldom show any allegiance to the African American community for fear of losing their precious contracts and media endorsements. Lacking an African-centered consciousness, they forget their heritage, the plight of the people they left behind, the condition of many of our neighborhoods, and the color of their skin. But when something goes wrong and they are kicked off their team, who do they come crying to? The African American community. As the most forgiving group of people in the world, we receive our prodigal sons with open arms, no matter how badly they abused and neglected us.

As a community, we must develop a plan to work with young athletes, male and female, as they are growing up. We must instill an African consciousness early in their young lives. We must teach them as babies that you never forget where you came from and that you must always give back your time, love, and money in return. This generates a positive cycle of achievement. Otherwise, we'll continue to experience brain drains and loss in general in our community. This positive cycle not only helps the race to step up higher, it makes the athlete a better person, a psychologically healthy person.

Many African American athletes are being cursed by the very success so many of us envy. Overnight rags to riches has short-circuited their brains. They seem driven by hormones, ego, and greed. Daily we hear of downfalls caused by drugs, incarceration, prostitution, irresponsible sex, domestic violence, and more. Apparently, being rich has not bought them the freedom that our people still desire.

Redefining Success

African American pro athletes, you must rethink what it means to be successful. Look around at your peers and how many have fallen to drug abuse and trouble with the law. Look at the retired athletes who are cash poor because they spent up all their money while they were in the game. Now ask yourself some questions:

- Can you read? Did you finish high school or college?
- What are you going to do once you leave your sport? Do you have a plan?
- What's your personal life like today? Do you have the image of success but your personal life is a disaster?
- Have you ever gone back to the old neighborhood to help a child? To give praise to former teachers? To honor your parents and pastor? To establish a business?
- Have you ever contributed financially to an African American organization?
- What are you doing to ensure that young athletes coming up in the system do not get caught in mental slavery?

Success is about more than making a lot of money. Success is about achieving an overall quality of life. Here are the components of success:

- Strong family life.
- Good friendships.
- Good health.
- Good education.
- Comfortable living conditions.
- Fulfilling church membership.
- Serving the community.
- Meaningful work.
- Strong investment portfolio.
- Cash in the bank.

If you've only got money, you're not yet successful. You must begin to work on all the other areas of your life to achieve true success.

One of the above criteria, "serving the community," is especially important for athletes to achieve peace of mind. You will help yourself only when you begin to help others. Professional African American athletes wield an unbelievable amount of financial clout. How about coming together with other athletes and community members to pool some of that money for the good of us all?

Former NBA All Star Isiah Thomas told BET commentator Charlie Neal that "he and a few others were definitely moving in that direction of unification of some of their money and intellectual wealth to purchase the right pro sports franchise."[1] Danny Manning, forward for the Phoenix Suns, invested $5 million in the purchase of the Arizona Diamondbacks.[2]

Magic Johnson, whose estimated wealth totals $100 million, is a rare example of a retired athlete who has managed to wield power in the business world. *USA Today* reports that

Magic Johnson is now making many fast break deals: He's still vice president and five percent owner of the Lakers. He's also an adviser to Mike Tyson. He's a spokesman and potential investor in the group headed by Michael Ovitz to bring an NFL expansion team to Los Angeles. His Magic Johnson theatres have been successful in Los Angeles, Houston, and Atlanta and planned expansion into six other major cities. His joint venture with Starbucks at an L.A. store has been a huge hit. Johnson is also a 50-50 partner in a TGI Friday's restaurant in Atlanta. His partnership in a proposed $100 million retail plaza in L.A.'s Crenshaw District, a mostly African American neighborhood.[3]

African American athletes, you have a responsibility to help elevate your race. We all do, but you have the clout. You could actually make it happen. Here are some things you can begin to do today to help us all:

- ◆ Mentor a young athlete.
- ◆ Be a role model. Stay clean.
- ◆ Go back to your old neighborhood and buy up all the vacant lots. Hire Black teens to keep them clean of garbage. Develop quality, low-income housing on those lots.

- Sponsor a scholarship.
- Talk to your Black peers in the pro sports world about doing the right thing and getting their lives in order.

As you begin to heal your mind and take action on behalf of your own race, you will achieve real success and freedom. You will no longer be a mental slave. There is nothing wrong with being rich, just keep your money in perspective. Financial wealth is only one part of the success formula, and to be honest, not even the most important part. Why do you think the Bible says "It is more blessed to give than to receive?"

Reason 22—The Desire for Instant Wealth

When was the last time a friend of yours won the lottery? Probably never. Another question: When was the last time your friend *played* the lottery? Probably a few minutes ago.

We want our money big and we want it today. It is better to live with money in this capitalist society than without, so we plan and dream and scheme for our share of the American pie. Instead of following all the recommendations I've presented in this book about pooling our financial resources to achieve wealth, some of us will continue to try and win the big one: The Lottery, Mega Bingo, The Numbers, Vegas.

One of us *might* win big, but given the astronomical odds against it, I assure you, the majority of us will win nothing. Would you open your window and throw out all your money? That's what you do every time you spend your hard earned dollars on a game of chance.

I challenge you to tally up all the money you've spent on these games over the past year. Not only didn't you win anything, you're probably broke besides. Some of our people are spending hundreds, even thousands of dollars in income, social security, pension, and welfare on these games with no success. If you spent, say, $500 this year on lottery tickets so far, here's some powerful things that you could have done with that money:

- Enrolled in classes at the local college.
- Given a grant to a struggling African American artist.
- Invested in a money market fund.
- Bought some blue chip stocks.
- Contributed to your church's building fund, or whatever special project is in the works.
- Saved toward a downpayment for a new home or apartment building.
- Started an investing club with family members or friends.
- Started a business.
- Repaired your home to raise its resale value.
- Saved toward a trip to an African nation.
- Provided seed money for a new African American business.
- Enrolled your children in a dance, music, or language class.

Need I go on? Money, like the mind, is a terrible thing to waste. We could be nation building with the billions of dollars that we waste each year on gambling.

If you must, go to a Gambler's Anonymous meeting and get yourself healed. Keep your money in your pocket. Then plan how you're going to build true wealth. In Southfield, Michigan, a group of 40 Black women, led by Barbara Talley, are pooling their resources and building wealth together. Reports *Black Enterprise*,

"Together, the group of women own 25,000 shares of Sara Lee common stock, a company that delivers big brand names such as Coach Bags, L'eggs Pantyhose, Playtex Bras, Champion Sport equipment, Hanes Underwear, Jimmy Dean

Sausage and Ball Park Franks...These sister investors, who turned heads at the gathering of 5,000—mostly white—investors represent a growing number of African Americans seeking to create wealth in the stock market."[1]

These African American women are proving that there is more than one way to beat the system at its own game.

When you die, what will your children inherit from you? Your debt and worthless lottery ticket stubs? Seldom do we pass anything of value to our children. If we change our wasteful habits and begin to save and invest now, on a regular basis, the inheritance picture for our children will improve.

We may want big money right away, but achieving wealth seldom happens overnight. Wealth building is a habit and a discipline. Every day you must tend to your accounts and curb your tendency to overspend, but as you'll see, it is worth the hard work.

Our desire for instant wealth is connected to our rampant spending on trendy clothes, luxury cars, vacations to Las Vegas, and more. We want what we think rich White people have. What we don't know is that the fancy clothes, big cars, and luxury vacations are seldom indulged in by the rich. Hollywood sold you that lie and you believed it because you watch so much TV. Many rich people shop at Sears and drive Hondas. They know that in order to build wealth you cannot spend up all your money.

Do you want to look wealthy, or do you really want to be wealthy? If you only want to keep up appearances, then keep doing what you're doing. But if you really want to be wealthy, then you're going to have to stop wasting your money on gambling, get your debt under control, build cash reserves, and invest. It's both simple and hard, especially if you've got a gambling problem or believe you need to keep up appearances.

To build wealth, it's going to take a lot of hard work and sacrifice. You're no stranger to hard work and sacrifice. You work hard on your job while the men at the top take home all the money. You sacrifice precious time that you could be spending with your family in order to make other people rich. You use up all your energy between the hours of 9:00am and 5:00pm to make the boss look good at his staff meetings. When will we Black folks wake up? If you can do it for them, you can do it for yourself. You owe it to yourself and your family to make your dreams of wealth come true. Take the necessary steps today. Vow to never again purchase a lottery ticket.

There are no shortcuts to success. However, you can shorten the time it will take to build wealth by pooling your money with like-minded people who have similar goals. If you attempt to become wealthy on your own, it's going to take twice as long.

Reason 23—Homosexuality

Men and women are like opposite poles of the magnet, thus, we come together in love and sexual relations. Ideally, we come together in marriage. So how is it that two men, or two women, can come together? Isn't that going against the natural law? It is certainly going against God's law.

I challenge you to find a scripture in any holy book of any religion that says two men or two women should come together as one. You're not going to find it. Where you will find it, though, is in man's sinful book.

Given our deep desire to be like everyone else, African Americans have put aside their upbringing and morals to come out of the closet. Homosexuality used to be a taboo in our community, but not any more. Today you'll find Black men walking down the street and holding hands in broad daylight. They appear to have no shame.

We hate the Ku Klux Klan and all White supremacy groups who advocate genocide and "ethnic cleansing," but really, who is killing us but ourselves? The African American homosexual lifestyle is a form of genocide that we are perpetrating upon ourselves. Two people of the same gender cannot produce children. Without children the race dies out. To make it clear, God tells us right up front in the Bible in Genesis, Chapter 1 what he intended regarding sexual relations. Like they say, God didn't make Adam and Steve, he made Adam and Eve. If you are involved in this lifestyle, I urge you to read your Bible and heed it. The price for disobedience is too great. Change your ways.

If you are a man, then be a man. Don't even try to be a woman because God did not make you that way. The same counsel goes for women—that is, be a woman.

And to all homosexuals everywhere, stop comparing your plight to ours. Being African American is not a choice. It is who we are. We couldn't hide in a closet even if we wanted to. Our skin color sets us apart from everyone else. On the other hand, homosexuality is a choice that you make and a lifestyle that you learn. My color is permanent, but you can change.

African Americans, please, refrain from homosexuality. Even if you are in jail, don't do it. Practice celibacy. Not having sex is not going to kill you. In fact, it will keep you alive. Seek God's face and change your ways to ensure your place in His eternity. Don't take my word for it. Read Genesis 18:16–33 and 19:1–29 and get a good look at what God Almighty did to a people who disobeyed Him.

Reason 24—Fear

According to the Bible, the only fear we are allowed to have is fear of Almighty God. Jesus said to his disciples, "Do not be afraid of those who kill the body but cannot afterward do anything worse. I will show you whom to fear: fear God, who, after killing, has the authority to throw into hell. Believe me, he is the one you must fear!"[1]

We are to trust that God will meet all of our needs. No matter where you are in life, fear no one but the Almighty for He will bring you through.

Yet, we do fear. We fear the unknown. We fear the thunder and lightening. We fear success, and we fear failure. We fear for our lives and we fear financial ruin.

Sometimes our fears are based on disasters that have happened to people we love. Our neighborhoods are often hotbeds of violence, drug dealing, gang wars, rape, murder, and mayhem. If you are a peace loving person, but do not have faith in God, it's enough to scare you to death.

Sometimes our fears are based on things that happened to our people in the past: slavery, the Great Depression, the world wars, Jim Crow discrimination and violence against African Americans, and the civil rights riots still affect us even as we turn the page to a new millennium.

Sometimes our fears are based on things that happened to us personally. If you were robbed, experienced financial setbacks in your business, lost your home, lost a child to violence, or got deathly sick, then you might be experiencing fear in your life. Still, the Bible says that we are only to fear God and nothing else. We are to trust that God will take care of us. He said that every hair on our heads are numbered and that He knows our name. He said that we are to care for nothing.

Either God is real or He isn't. Either the Word of God is true, or it's a lie. I believe that God is more real than what I can see, hear, taste, touch, or smell, and that the Word of God is absolutely true. That means, I must trust God with every fiber of my being when it comes to my safety and security. You must know without a doubt that God has got your back, front, and all around. You are safe and secure.

We fear the unknown, but truly, if we knew ahead of time what lay before us in the future, we might not have the strength to move forward. We might get scared into paralysis. It's a good thing that we don't know our future. Do not fear the unknown, give thanks for it.

In *Stride Toward Freedom*, Dr. King explained that White people act the way they do often out of fear. He says that "There is not only the job of freeing the Negro from the bondage of segregation but also the responsibility of freeing his white brothers from the bondage of fears concerning integration."[2]

The Bible says that perfect love casts out all fear. Thus, when you feel fear, think about the people you love. Don't give into the fear, give into the love. And above all, pray to your Protector. Think of God as a security blanket. Babies love their blankets because they make them feel safe. Let God wrap His arms around you. Stay in prayer and know that you are safe. There is nothing to fear.

As for your dreams, there's no time like the present to go for it. Don't let fear paralyze you. Take action today, even if it's a tiny step like going to the library to take out a book.

Don't let anyone discourage you from pursuing your dream. Those who criticize the loudest are often the most afraid.

I wrote the following poem to help you overcome your fear. Commit it to memory and remember that God is with you always.

Fear

Man's greatest enemy is fear.

It will break you down and cause a tear.

Do not be afraid of anything;

There are some things you must respect.

Weigh all decisions that's best for you.

No matter how tough the decision,

Make it! Stick with it!

Don't be wishy washy

Learn to say - NO! Most will understand.

Have your opinion. Others do.

The key to success is to conquer fear in total.

Fear no one but the Almighty.

Copyright 1978 Jimmy Dumas

You were placed here for a purpose and you and the Almighty know your dreams. Pursue it now and participate in the Damnedest Phenomena, that is the complete turn around of African American people.

Afterword

"The less we have the less we keep" and "the more we have the less we keep"!! This is the damnedest phenomena that has ever beset any race of mankind on the face of the earth. One would think a group of people, or anyone who has been denied everything from existence, would want to keep and hold onto something once it has presented itself. African Americans will not and do not. Why not?

By all rights, African Americans should be the wealthiest people on the face of the earth, especially if they adhered to the above theory. If we equate suffering and denial with accomplishing and refusing to be without because someone has denied them, we should be wealthy. The logical approach would be to hold onto everything that one has accomplished as the chains of suppression were being broken. Eventually, with this mentality one will not find oneself in a position of constant dependency upon someone else for your well being and survival, especially a mere man. Having been denied everything, wouldn't it stand to reason that African Americans would hold onto everything that she and her people have accomplished? This should include our history and our heritage.

Doesn't it stand to reason that once you have been denied that which was held near and dear to your souls, one would definitely make it his or her life's ambition to hold onto it once it was achieved? A reasonable and prudent person would. African Americans hold onto your history, legacy, heritage, your dreams, your money for a little while, hold on. A breakthrough will come in the morning. Hold On! Why Not!

African Americans have held on from the days of slavery to little or no income to earning in excess of $5.00 per hour. It may not seem like much but it far exceeds where we came from. Hold on to this and any other income that you have earned. Make it work for you, your community and your people.

Having been denied everything from basic reading to writing, entrance through the front door, a good job, and a cool drink of water on a hot day and many of these denials still linger today. Hold on any how, a Breakthrough is coming. Having been denied all of these things, then and now, but constantly achieving against great odds, why not hold onto the many things that you and your race have accomplished. Hold onto your heritage. Hold onto your dreams and desires. Hold onto your income and watch your dreams and desires become a reality. Hold onto education. Hold onto family. Hold onto Christianity. Above all hold onto each other as a team creating strength and common bond that is undeniable. Above all, "HOLD ON!"

It never fails, if you continue to "HOLD ON" till your last grasp, help will come. In some form or another, you will receive divine intervention to get you through your ordeal and onto your dream. Even though you may think the ship is going down, don't give up, grab a piece of the ship, a board or a plank or splinter and hold on, help will come. "HOLD ON."

The information presented in the previous pages was not intended to degrade or poke fun at African Americans. My goal was to inspire, motivate, and challenge you to new heights in your quest for respect and your rightful place in the American mainstream.

If I made you think, become angry, or ashamed of yourself, that is good. Hopefully you will use the uncomfortable feelings to change your life for the better. My hope is that African Americans will finally wake up and realize the economic power we have among us. If only we would come together in unity. We are the only race of people on the face of the earth without a common goal, common bond, or common project. If, after reading this book, a family, couple, or community group decides to buy an old house, renovate it, and then sell it at a profit, then I will have accomplished my goal.

During the '60s and '70s, we had a level of awareness. We understood our plight and the solutions needed to resolve them. Across the country, African Americans joined in the fight for freedom and equal opportunities. We were passionate about our cause. With all the setbacks we are seeing in civil rights legislation, we must become vigilant once again. This time, let us not look to the government or White people to save us. We're strong and we're rich. Let us take care of our own. Thank God and Amen.

Endnotes

Open Letter to African Americans

1. Congress of National Black Churches, Brochure and Visions, Fall/Winter 1997, "Origin and Purpose."

2. Charles H. Wesley, *International Library of Negro Life and History*, Introduction (Miami: Publishers Company, Inc., 1968), p. ix.

Reason 1—Lack of Unity

1. Maulana Karenga, *Introduction to Black Studies* (Los Angeles: Kawaida Publications, 1984), p. 86.

2. "Democrats Energize Black Vote," *USA Today*, (Arlington, VA: Gannett Corporation, 11/2/98), p. 9A.

3. Wesley, p. 64.

4. US Census Bureau, www.census.gov/population/ESTS/ nation/intfile3-1.txt, 8/8/98.

Reason 2—Poor Money Management

1. US Census Bureau, www.census.gov/Press-Release-CB98/176.HTML, 9/24/98.

2. Wesley, pp. 62, 64.

3. Dennis Kimbro and Napoleon Hill, *Think and Grow Rich: A Black Choice* (New York: Fawcett Columbine Books, 1991), p. 223.

4. "Long Term Young Child Poverty Trends: Alarming Growth, Changing Demographics, Working Families in Poverty,"

Columbia School of Public Health (National Center for Children in Poverty, http://cpmcnet.columbia.edu/dept/nccp/reports/longterm.html).

5. "Real Estate," *Black Enterprise*, 8/98, p. 96.

6. Gregory J. Reed, *Economic Empowerment Through the Church*, Neighborhood Revitalization (Michigan: Zondervan Publishers, 1994), pp. 82–83.

7. "Real Estate," *Black Enterprise*, 8/98, p. 96.

8. "Real Estate," *Jet Magazine* (Chicago: Johnson Publishing Co., 11/20/98), p 4.

9. "Automobiles," *USA Today* (Arlington, VA: Gannett Corporation, 1/8/99), p. 14B.

10. Wesley, pp. 62, 64.

11. Derek T. Dingle, "B.E. Industrial/Service 100," *Black Enterprise*, 7/98, p.106.

12. Sherri A. McGee, "Making It, Individuality without Compromise," *Black Enterprise*, 7/98, p. 30.

13. Ibid., p. 30.

14. "Architects of the Next Millennium," *Black Enterprise*, 6/98, p. 101.

15. Karenga, p. 278.

16. US Census Bureau, www.census/gov/Pres-Release/CB98/176.HTML, 9/24/98.

17. Jacobs, Siegel, Quiram, *"Profile of the Nation*, Debt," (Texas: Information Plus Publisher, 1998), pp. 86, 87.

Reason 3—Lack of Education

1. Wesley, p 164.

2. Ibid., p 164.

3. US Census Bureau, www.census.gov/Pres-Release/CB98/176.HTML, 9/24/98.

4. Wesley, p. 166.

5. Ibid., p. 166.

Reason 4—Lack of Discipline

1. Jawanza Kunjufu, *Developing Positive Self Images and Discipline in Black Children,* (Chicago: African American Images, 1984), p. 52.

Reason 5—Welfare

1. *Happenings*, Alabama Department of Human Resources, Vol. XVIII (December 1996), p. 3.

Reason 6—Teen Pregnancy

1. Cliff Schimmels, *How to Help Your Child Survive and Thrive in Public Schools* (New Jersey: Fleming H. Revel Co.,) p. 158.

2. Ibid, p. 140.

3. Martin Luther King, Jr., "Advice for Living," *Ebony* (Chicago: Johnson Publishing Company, 1/95), p. 50.

Reason 7—Drugs

1. "Warning Signs Indicate Drug Abuse," *Mobile Register* (Mobile, AL: 1/12/99), p. 2D.
2. Reed, p. 94.

Reason 8—Lack of Morals

1. Exodus 20:1-17, *The Book* (Wheaton, IL: Tyndale House Publishers, Inc., 1971), pp. 82–83.
2. Ibid., p. 1192.
3. Wesley, p. 236.
4. King, "Advice for Living," *Ebony*, 1/95, p. 50.
5. Kimbro, p. 196.

Reason 9—The Jinx of Slavery

1. Psalms 37:1–2, 9–11, *The Holy Bible* (Nashville: Holman Bible Publishers, 1982), p. 929.
2. Kimbro, p. 274.

Reason 10—The Crisis Between African American Men and Women

1. Begun, Blair, & Quiram, *Women's Changing Roles*, (Texas: Information Plus Publishers, 1998), pp. 52–53.
2. Ibid., p. 82.

Reason 11—Lack of Spiritual Vision

1. Kunjufu, p. 27.
2. Wesley, p. 46.

3. Martin L. King Jr., *Stride Toward Freedom* (New York: Harper & Brothers, 1958), p. 208.

4. Wesley, p. 46.

Reason 12—Confusion About the Purpose of African American Sororities and Fraternities

1. *National Directory of African American Organizations 1998-2000*, p. 3.

2. "Architects of the Next Millennium," *Black Enterprise,* 6/98, p. 216.

Reason 13—Lack of Investigative African American Media

1. J.L. White & T. A. Parham, *The Psychology of Blacks* (New Jersey: Prentice Hall, 1990), p. 99.

2. Kunjufu, pp. 22–23.

Reason 14—Lack of Business Resources

1. Wesley, pp. 60, 62.

2. "Wanted: Black Entrepreneurs," *Advisor* (Alabama: Retirement Systems of Alabama, 2/99, Vol. XXIV, No. 8), p. 3.

Reason 16—Interracial Marriage

1. King, "Advice for Living," *Ebony*, 1/95, pp. 49–50.

Reason 17—Poor Health

1. Norma Chappell, "African American Health Is Code Blue," *Upscale*, Dec./Jan. 1999, p. 60.

2. Ibid., p. 60.

3. Kimbro, p. 36.

4. Chappell, p. 60.

5. Ibid., pp. 60, 61.

6. Alfred "Coach" Powell, *Message 'N A Bottle: The 40oz Scandal* (Chicago: Renaissance Press, 1996).

Reason 20—Ignorance About African American Contributions to Science and Technology

1. Wesley, p. 58.

2. Ibid., p. 58.

3. Ibid., p. 58.

4. Ibid., p. 58.

Reason 21—Lack of Support from African American Athletes

1. Charlie Neal's Interview of Isiah Thomas, BET Television, October 1, 1998

2. "Manning: Investments by D'Backs Sound Move," *USA Today*, 2/3/99, p. 6C.

3. David Leon Moore, "Magic is all business," *USA Today*, pp. C1, C2.

Reason 22—The Desire for Instant Wealth

1. "Moneywise," *Black Enterprise*, 2/99, p. 66.

Reason 24—Fear

1. *The Living Bible*, (Wheaton, IL: Tyndale House Publishers, 1971), p. 1028.

2. King, *Stride Toward Freedom*, p. 206.

NOTES

NOTES

NOTES

NOTES

NOTES

NOTES

NOTES

NOTES

NOTES

NOTES

NOTES

NOTES

NOTES

NOTES